EARLY
STAFFORDSHIRE POTTERY

The Faber Monographs on
Pottery and Porcelain

Edited by W. B. HONEY

★

★

OTHER TITLES TO FOLLOW

C. TEAPOT. WHITE SALTGLAZE WARE PAINTED IN ENAMEL
COLOURS WITH CHINESE FIGURES. H. 7⅜ in. ABOUT 1755.
Victoria and Albert Museum
See page 33

EARLY
STAFFORDSHIRE POTTERY

by

BERNARD RACKHAM

FABER AND FABER
24 Russell Square
London

*First published in mcmli
by Faber and Faber Limited
24 Russell Square London W.C. 1
Printed in Great Britain by
R. MacLehose and Company Limited
The University Press Glasgow*

To
GORDON MITCHELL FORSYTH

FOREWORD

The subject of Mr. Rackham's book is one of great historical importance. Considered in relation to the whole field of ceramic studies and usages in the seventeenth and eighteenth centuries it stands for nothing less than a revolution, whose outcome was the development of the English cream-coloured and white earthenware bodies, and a triumph for the English potter in the world market. But in one respect it stood for a great loss. The Staffordshire productions were technically much more efficient than the delftware and faïence which were then the current types of useful ware, and these with their delightful decoration were now driven out of existence.

But as compensation, the rise of Staffordshire brought a wealth of new and interesting types which are the subject of this book, produced incidentally, on the way, as it were, to the establishment of cream-colour. As first evidence of a new craftsmanlike pride came the slipware; then, as evidence of a Chinese-inspired impulse towards refinement came the Elers ware, leading eventually to the salt-glazed stoneware, plain and coloured, the 'Astbury' and 'Whieldon' and 'Ralph Wood' wares, and many other types of which Mr. Rackham will write in the course of this book.

W. B. H.

ACKNOWLEDGEMENTS

The author wishes to thank very warmly many former colleagues and other friends who have kindly helped him with answers to enquiries or with valuable suggestions and information; among them he would like to mention, besides the Editor of this series of Monographs, Mr. William King of the British Museum and Mr. Arthur Lane of the Victoria and Albert Museum, Mr. Geoffrey Bemrose, Mr. Gordon Forsyth, Mr. Bernard Leach, and Mr. M. A. Palmer. He is also much indebted to Mr. J. E. Dixon, Mr. A. J. B. Kiddell, Mr. and Mrs. Lowy, and Mr. and Mrs. T. M. Ragg for their kindness in allowing him to reproduce in the illustrations specimens from their collections; he is indebted for similar courtesies to the Corporation of Bedford and the Trustees of the Cecil Higgins Museum, and to the authorities of the many other museums named in the titles to the plates.

CONTENTS

xiii

ILLUSTRATIONS

COLOUR PLATES

MONOCHROME PLATES

ILLUSTRATIONS

1

ORIGINS AND RECORDS

The cluster of towns in North Staffordshire commonly known as The Potteries and now amalgamated to form the municipality of Stoke-on-Trent has a position unique in Europe. In earlier times and in most countries the potter's craft was usually carried on in a small way wherever suitable beds of clay were at hand; the output was intended only to supply the needs of the surrounding neighbourhood. England was no exception to this rule. Methods of production and materials employed in these small potworks were in principle much the same, in whatever part of the country they were situated; archaeological research continues to disclose the existence during the Middle Ages of very many small kilns, previously unknown, from Lancashire and Yorkshire in the north to Sussex in the south and Devon in the west, and it is likely that many more existed of which clear evidence has yet to be found. In many of these, traditional medieval methods producing rough earthenware usually covered with a lead glaze continued in practice down to the eve of the present day, when one after another, as small rural handicrafts, they proved unequal to the demands of modern culture and succumbed in the struggle.

The same story of the extinction of traditional medieval potteries was repeated on the Continent. Trade with the East brought within the reach of Europe wares produced by other methods and attaining a standard previously unknown and for long after beyond the powers of Western potters; but this competition imposed upon those who wished to survive the adoption, if not of Oriental technique in its entirety, at least of methods which could produce a passable substitute for the greatly superior wares of the East. Thus came into being in the fifteenth and sixteenth centuries the tin-glazed maiolica, faïence or delft (for the terms are virtually synonymous) of Italy, Spain and other countries and at a later date, the various kinds of European porcelain; in nearly every country these innovations brought about the decline, if not the total extinction of the indigenous wares. A similar fate befell the minor potteries scattered over England, but in a different way: the tin-glazed technique did indeed invade this country, but failed to hold its own and was abandoned even sooner than elsewhere. Porcelain works were also established, but their survival

B 1

became precarious, and depended at last on compromise with methods which were the outcome of a curious train of development.

One region alone in England presents an exception to the usual sequence of events. The potteries of Staffordshire not only held their own against the invaders, but by adroit adaptation to new social conditions and adoption of new processes of manufacture succeeded at last in extending their supremacy throughout Europe and even in some measure over most parts of the world. And this supremacy they attained not by the total abandonment of methods handed down from the Middle Ages, as happened so generally on the Continent, but by a gradual modification of these methods which won for them complete victory in the competitive struggle. Not only were the smaller provincial potworks, based like those of Staffordshire itself on medieval tradition, driven from the field, but the innovators who had established delft manufacture on English soil were compelled to retire; in the end a shattering blow was struck at those potteries abroad in which tin-glazing was employed, and even the porcelain factories were not unaffected. The ceramic industries of the Continent were constrained in the nineteenth century to accept as the price of survival methods dictated to a large extent from Staffordshire.

It is interesting to inquire into the reasons for this advance of the Staffordshire potters from an insignificant to a dominant position. Initially these potters had no peculiar skill unshared by their fellow-craftsmen in other parts of England. In London and its region, in York, the Midlands and East Anglia, pots were made in medieval times which, for all their rudimentary simplicity of technique, have great aesthetic virtues and, within the limits of their materials, a considerable degree of efficiency. Moreover, North Staffordshire is not among the districts which can show evidence of ceramic production of high standard till long after the close of the Middle Ages. This is a matter which calls for explanation.

Special circumstances put Staffordshire in a position of advantage. These were in part recognized by Simeon Shaw of Burslem, the earliest historian of The Potteries. An adequate supply of fuel is a necessity of the manufacture, and in the seventeenth century there was throughout England, owing to various causes, a danger of serious shortage of the wood which at that time was still in use for firing potters' kilns. Coal was now being exploited for fuel as an alternative to wood, and any district which could provide ready to hand not only clay but also coal was obviously at an advantage where making pots was concerned. This is the position in North Staffordshire; the district can show beds of clay differing in quality, some superior in plasticity, others more refractory—possessing, that is, a higher degree of resistance to heat, and capable of producing various effects of colour when fired; alongside these beds of clay in immediate proximity are carboniferous strata yielding ample supplies of coal, so that the cost of fuel is reduced to a minimum. Another advantage of the situation was easy access, at first by packhorse highways and later by the canal which the manufacturers found it worth while to construct, to the ports of the Mersey and Dee and, through Willington Quay on the Trent, to the Humber; by these routes the potters were able cheaply to distribute their wares, when once their good qualities were recognized, throughout the kingdom and even beyond, and also to import accessory materials, such as flints and certain kinds of clay not found in their own neighbourhood, which enabled them as time went on to improve the quality and to widen the variety of their products.

For our knowledge of the early history of the Staffordshire potteries we are dependent chiefly on two sources, apart from evidences that can be gleaned from the examination of the wares themselves. The earlier of two printed accounts is that given by the seventeenth-century antiquary Dr. Robert Plot (the first Keeper of the Ashmolean Museum) in his *Natural History of Staffordshire*, published in 1686. This author visited the district and gives an account based on his own observations and inquiries as to the methods of manufacture then followed, the clays used, and the various wares produced; his exposition has on the face of it an air of veracity, and its reliability is borne out by comparison with the wares which still survive from his time. Not so much can be said of the writer who next after him, at a long interval, turned his attention to recording in print what he knew of the industry; for much of our knowledge of the personal history of the eighteenth-century potters and of the development of the art in their hands our only source is *The History of the Staffordshire Potteries* by Simeon Shaw, already mentioned, which was published in 1829. Our confidence in this writer's assertions is shaken not only by the slovenly and ill-coordinated manner in which the facts and events are set down but also by statements which can be shown to be palpably untrue; for instance, a tyg (or mug) which from its description can be recognized beyond doubt as one of a very distinctive class made at Wrotham in Kent, is claimed as a local production, and stoneware exactly corresponding, as described, with tankards unquestionably coming from the kilns of Fulham or Lambeth is similarly spoken of as an early Staffordshire type.

Shaw asserts that coarse pottery was made in the sixteenth century at Golden Hill, which is situated at the extreme northern end of the district, and that 'in 1600' there were three manufactories of coarse brown pottery at Penkhull, a place close to Stoke-on-Trent. More reliable evidence of the early establishment of the craft in the neighbourhood is provided by occupational names in certain Court Rolls of the fourteenth century. Less equivocal information can be got from legal documents such as leases and wills; of these there is no lack from the early years of the seventeenth century onwards. Burslem was now the principal centre of the pottery manufacture, and so it remained until the period of expansion in the nineteenth century which spread the industry over the entire region from Golden Hill near the Cheshire boundary, beyond Tunstall, in the north to Longton and Meir Lane End in the south. Lastly mention may be made of a manuscript statement drawn up by Josiah Wedgwood in 1765 as to the condition of the industry at Burslem and Hanley early in the eighteenth century; this document[1] gives a list of potters showing the nature of the goods they made.

[1] Printed by Josiah C. Wedgwood, *Staffordshire Pottery and its History*, London, n.d., pp. 48 ff.

2

SLIP WARE

The earliest surviving wares which can with certainty be attributed to the Staffordshire Potteries belong to the class known as 'slip ware', from the process by which they are decorated. The types of 'body' in which they are made vary, but by far the commonest is a clay firing to a moderately hard close-grained earthenware with a buff surface resembling chamois-leather in colour; examples are also sometimes found in a clay which comes from the kiln a warm red. The decoration is done in clay of various colours mixed with water to the creamy consistency known as 'slip' and applied to the surface of the wares when these have been allowed to dry to a leather-hard condition. The slip was laid on by pouring out of a spouted jug or can; where narrow lines or dots were to be produced the liquid was passed through quills of different sizes fitted into an opening in the side of the slip-can, whilst the flow was controlled by closing or opening a hole in the top which could be covered by the thumb of the potter. The final procedure in preparing the wares for the kiln was the application of the lead glaze. Lead ore (galena) ground to a powder was 'finely sifted and strewed' (in Dr Plot's words) on the ware, or dusted on with a rag; the iron almost always present as an impurity in the ore gave the transparent glaze so produced a more or less strong yellow tone, causing the underlying clays to appear cream-coloured, buff, warm red or rich dark brown consistently with the colours acquired by them in the firing (1). The dishes which are the most conspicuous and the commonest among the slip wares are as a rule glazed on the upper surface only, the under side showing the buff or red of the body without this heightening of colour; where the glaze has stopped short or failed to take, it is sometimes possible also to see the tones assumed by the other clays when not intensified or modified by the glassy coating.

The dishes, mostly circular, decorated by the process described show great variety in design. A common shape, usually about 15 or 18 inches in diameter, shows a flat middle without any kind of foot-rim on the back, rising by a curve to the inner edge of a wide, flat, nearly horizontal rim which is trimmed with a knife to a bevel at its edge.

(1) *Plate* 19.

5

The rim often displays a name trailed on in slip in large capitals (at the lower extremity when the dish is set up on edge on a dresser); the name occupies a space reserved in the pattern which covers the rest of the rim, usually a trellis of closely-set dark brown and red lines laid one over the other, the red uppermost. The designs filling the middle of the dish show by their variety great fertility of imagination. Some are heraldic—the lion (1), alone or with the unicorn, from the Royal arms, a double-headed spread eagle, a fleur-de-lis; these, like the 'Pelican in her Piety' (2), the mermaid (3), and Saint George and the Dragon, were doubtless prompted by the signs of inns, as was also the king's head, crowned. The king in question can in some cases be deduced to be Charles II from the cipher appended to the highly schematic portrait, in conformity with the style of wig and costume which is seen complete where the whole figure is shown. Dishes occur with the head of William III also; the type was continued till the time of Queen Anne, as shown by a dish with her cipher, dated 1712. The bust or figure of Catherine of Braganza sometimes accompanies her consort (4). Some ambitious examples put a strain on the decorative possibilities of the technique by attempting to display the Royal achievement entire, with shield, crown, garter, supporters and motto.

The commonest method was to draw the outline of the design by trailing a line of slip made from a clay with a strong iron content firing to dark brown, which after being allowed to dry was usually picked out with small dots of white slip dropped along it; in some cases patches of deep buff or reddish-brown clay have been laid first, to be enclosed afterwards with such an outline—for the body of a lion, for instance, or a flower (5), or the coat of a royal personage. Quite a different and a very striking effect results where the surface of a dish or pot has been entirely coated with a dark slip (the colour of treacle when seen through the yellow glaze) and the design trailed on it in plain white line (6) or white and buff (7); such linear designs are sometimes interspersed with small applied discs or pads of white clay, either stuck on or dropped from a slip-can, to receive an impression from a wooden stamp cut so as to produce a rosette or star ornament in relief (8). There are cases where the dark-on-light and light-on-dark are combined on a single vessel, as in the upper and lower zones of a goblet or a posset-pot; a very lively effect is the result (9). In one small class not often met with a slip has been used of a colour which appears under the glaze a greyish green; where this has been applied in broad

---

(1) *Plate* 2; (2) *Plate* 3; (3) *Colour-Plate* A; (4) *Plate* 4; (5) *Plate* 10A; (6) *Plates* 8, 9A, 11A; (7) *Plates* 19, 22B; (8) *Plates* 9B 7, 18; (9) *Plate* 11B.

patches it sometimes shows the imprint of meshes of a coarse fabric used to press it on to the surface of the pot (an example is the cup at Cambridge (1) with elaborate wing handles of which the form seems to be derived from a Netherlandish wineglass of the seventeenth century); pieces showing this characteristic are probably all the work of one potter, perhaps Thomas Toft (it is found on the Adam and Eve dish mentioned on p. 10 (2)). In another unusual class the white slip decoration is trailed directly on a warm red 'body'; the same red clay is also used as a slip on a white ground (3).

Dr. Plot in the account of his visit to Burslem in 1677 speaks of the use of slips of various colours for painting but has nothing to say of the character of the designs produced. He does however mention a process to which some of the finest examples of slip ware owe their attractiveness. He describes how two colours, white and red, are 'broken' with a wire brush 'much after the manner they do when they marble paper, and then cloud them with a pencil when they are dry'; by this method the irregular marbled surfaces were produced which are often of extraordinary beauty (4). In some cases it appears as if the two clays had been laid on the surface in patches, perhaps with a brush, in a fairly fluid condition and then caused to intermingle and flow into one another merely by tilting the dish first one way and then another. Slip in a fluid state was also used to produce the lovely feather-patterns which are seen on dishes and with most beautiful effectiveness on mugs, jars and posset-pots; horizontal parallel lines are laid—dark-on-light or light-on-dark—and then traversed while still wet with a comb or with a stick or other pointed tool moved upward and downward in alternation, the resultant pattern having the appearance of feathers or fronds laid over the surface (5), or of ladder-like stripes (6). In a mug at Cambridge dated 1694 this technique is used to fill the outlines of a tulip design. (7).

Such decorations as these, and simple patterns of spots and trailed lines, straight or sinuous, were employed to enliven wares made for ordinary domestic use; they continued in favour long after the end of the seventeenth century. Nor were they confined to Staffordshire; they survived into the nineteenth century in other pottery centres in the Midlands and North where Staffordshire slip ware was imitated, such as Black Burton in Yorkshire and Ticknall in Derbyshire. The more elaborate pictorial designs described on an earlier page were doubtless reserved as a rule for pieces made to celebrate special occasions such as births, betrothals and weddings, or for service at festive gatherings.

(1) *Plate* 11B; (2) *Plate* 6; (3) *Plates* 12, 13; (4) *Plates* 1, 18; (5) *Plate* 15; (6) *Plate* 9A; (7) *Plate* 14.

In these categories we find, besides the dishes already mentioned, tygs (mugs with several handles for easy circulation in a drinking party), posset-pots with lids for serving hot beverages (1), jugs, jars with lids, egg-stands (2), bleeding-bowls (3), and the rare vessels shaped as owls, with head detachable for use as a cup, their plumage well imitated in slip (4). Teapots of slip ware are rare, owing partly to frequent exposure to risk of damage in washing-up; when tea came within the purchasing power of the country folk for whom slip ware was made, a finer and more suitable type of earthenware had been evolved of which more will be said. Models of cradles were made to be given to parents on the birth of a child. A variant of the round platter is an oblong baking-dish with rounded corners resembling in shape a gardener's trug without its handle.

A group apart among the dishes and plates of Staffordshire slip ware consists of those in which the slip 'painting' is laid over a pre-existing design in raised outline. This is produced by shaping the dish on a convex mould in which the design has been incised or impressed before firing; in the majority of cases the linear design is for the most part reinforced with 'milling' or dots apparently impressed with roulettes ('runners') of various gauge; small stamps have been used for rosettes or discs in the intervals of the linear design (5). The technique is clearly revealed by the survival of several such moulds, complete or fragmentary. One such, in the British Museum, is inscribed on the back: 'William Bird made this mould in the Year of Our Lord 1751.' (6). This mould displays a figure of a man in a wide-brimmed hat and frock coat drawn with an economy of detail admirably suited to the technique; it was used for a slip ware dish in the Manchester Art Gallery. After shaping in the mould the raised outlines of the design have been traced over with lines of slip, and broad patches have been laid for details of the costume in the same manner as in the wares which are painted 'freehand'; as in these also, the application of glaze on the upper side only of the dish completes preparation for the single firing in the kiln. This moulding technique is peculiar to Staffordshire; it does not seem to have been used in the small potteries elsewhere in England which produced slip ware in the seventeenth and eighteenth centuries.

These moulded relief wares fall into two readily distinguishable groups, an earlier and a later. No dated examples are known of the earlier group, but the evidence of their designs points to a period before the Civil War; a plate in the Fitzwilliam Museum, Cambridge,

---

(1) *Plate* 7; (2) *Plate* 23B; (3)*Plate* 10B; (4) *Plate* 16; (5) *Plate* 21; (6) *Plates* 22A, 23A.

is decorated with a mounted trooper with sword and pistol, in the conical hat and 'bombasted' trunk hose which began their vogue in the time of Shakespeare (1). The picture in the middle panel of another plate in the same museum points to a like conclusion as to date—a man and woman in costume of the same period wrangling over possession of a pair of breeches; it has to be remembered however that this design is probably based on a woodcut which may have served as a copy some time after its publication: potters in an out-of-the-way country district cannot be expected always to be up-to-date. Initials on a dish of this class in the British Museum are perhaps those of Ralph Simpson of Burslem (*b.* 1651, *d.* 1724) (2). The edge in these earlier wares is finished with a decorative frilling which in certain instances has been produced by repeated impressions of a small corrugated shell (3); in the later group the edge is notched or milled by means of a 'runner'—perhaps not merely for decoration but for the practical purpose of giving a better hold for pastry when the dish is used for baking a covered pie. On these later moulded dishes (4), which are as a rule saucer-shaped without a rim, there are dated examples showing that they were being made throughout the first half of the eighteenth century (William Bird's mould is dated 1751).

The more elaborate slip-painted wares were made as much with a decorative as with a utilitarian intention, often doubtless to celebrate such family events as a birthday, a betrothal or wedding. Inscriptions are of common occurrence, frequently of a kind appropriate to gifts. 'The best is not too good for you' is a favourite declaration (5); on a posset-pot in the Hanley Museum these words are combined with the name ROBBORT WOOD (6), and on a fine example in the Harris Museum, Preston, they are followed by the statement that 'Daniel Steel made mee 1711'. Sometimes the inscriptions express loyalty to the throne. One such informs us that 'George Ward made this cup and so no more but God bless the Queen and all her parleme [*sic*]'; another, on a posset-pot dated 1708, names John Meir as its maker and couples 'prence Gorge' with his consort as the object of benediction. Gift pieces are clearly indicated where such words as 'Mary Oumfaris your cup 1678' are accompanied by initials (in this case RM) or a second name ('William Ley 1715 Elizabeth Ley her cup', in the Brighton Museum). A posset-pot in the Victoria and Albert Museum has an inscription telling us clearly that it was made by Thomas Dakin for Mary Sculltharp in 1710, but this statement

---

(1) *Plate* 20; (2) *Plate* 25 (*compare p.* 10 *below*); (3) *Plate* 21; (4) *Plate* 24; (5) *Plate* 7; (6) *Plate* 17.

is followed by the words 'her friend AB' which can only be explained by assuming that it was AB, too shy to divulge his or her name in full, who gave the order for it to the potter.

In many cases it is not clear whether the names inscribed are those of the maker or the destined owner. Where the name is known to be that of a potter there is a strong presumption in favour of the first alternative, even if there is no explicit assertion of authorship such as those already cited. The names of potters thus inconclusively inscribed include William, Ralph (1) and John Simpson, Joseph Glass, and Richard Meir (alias Mare); of these Glass is stated in Wedgwood's note[1] to have made 'Clowdy a sort of dishes painted with diff't color'd slips' (that is, marbled ware) about the beginning of the eighteenth century at Hanley. Evidence has come to light in recent years to prove that the initials S.M. seen on several dishes of the moulded outline class formerly attributed to Samuel Meir are actually those of Samuel Malkin of Burslem, who died in 1741 (2); a dish of this kind with a clock-face design bears his name in full, and potsherds of the same kind were found on a site known to be that of his factory.

Among all the slip-painted wares the best known and among the best in design are those bearing the name Thomas Toft; they are not confined to dishes but include also a loving-cup (in the Yorkshire Museum, York) with busts of Charles II, which bears also the name Elisabeth Poot, and a jug. Most of the dishes with Toft's name conform to the broad-rimmed type with painting on a pale buff ground and a close trellis-pattern interrupted by the inscribed panel; one, in the Fitzwilliam Museum, is in several ways exceptional, having decoration on a dark brown ground in trailed slips which include the greenish-grey already mentioned; in the middle are figures of Adam and Eve, common enough on English delft ware but seemingly unique on slip ware; Toft's name on the rim is in a panel set among tulips and pomegranates instead of the usual trellis (3). Only less numerous than the dishes inscribed 'Thomas Toft', and similar in general character of design though inferior in execution, are those with the name of another member of the Toft family, Ralph. Neither Thomas nor Ralph is recorded in any list as a potter, and although the latter had property in 1666 at Shelton (part of Hanley), the only mention of the former, in the same Hearth Tax Roll, is under Stanley, near Leek, some four miles from the pottery district; in neither case however is there clear evidence that these persons did not make pottery. The dates (where present) on inscribed pieces range

[1] See p. 4 above.

---

(1) *Plates* 5, 25; (2) *Plate* 24; (3) *Plate* 6.

A. DISH. SLIP WARE. DIAM. $17\frac{1}{4}$ in. ABOUT 1660-1680.
Victoria and Albert Museum
See page 6

from 1671 to 1683 for Thomas Toft and from 1676 to 1683 for Ralph—all dates, it will be noted, later than those given in the Roll, and allowing of the possibility of a change of residence in the interval.

The inconclusiveness of these facts has prompted some question of the validity of arguments drawn from the wares themselves in favour of the Tofts as their makers rather than the persons for whom they were made. In relief of such doubts may be adduced pieces on which Thomas Toft's name is found in company with others. The cup at York has already been mentioned; a parallel is provided by an imposing dish dated 1671 in the Chester Museum with the Royal arms which bears Toft's name in full as well as those of Filep and Elesabeth Heves, for whom presumably it was made. On a lion and unicorn dish in the Victoria and Albert Museum the initials TL accompanying his name might, it is true, be those of the maker; the circumstance that the Tofts' names occupy precisely the same relative position as those of potters such as the Simpsons must not be pressed, in view of the fact that the same can be said of some names of women, who are most unlikely to have been potters. On the other hand, the number of dishes and vessels surviving with Thomas Toft's name on them—in the Fitzwilliam Museum alone there are five—suggests that the inscription can hardly be a mere mark of dedication or ownership; the same holds good of the Ralph Toft dishes, hardly less numerous, and the fact that in at least two cases the designs on these (a rampant lion and a mermaid) duplicate in a greatly inferior manner those on dishes with the name of Thomas seems to point to the same conclusion.

Akin to the slip-painted wares in the materials used but differing in technique is a small class dating from the eighteenth century in which the decoration is effected by a method known in many parts of the world and in much earlier times; from the fact that it was first described—in writing—in books on Italian pottery this kind of ware is known by an Italian word, as *sgraffiato* ('scratched') ware. The process consists in laying on the surface of the vessel a coating of clay differing in colour from that of the 'body' and then scratching or cutting the decoration, before firing, through the coat so as to lay bare the underlying body; as in the case of slip painting, the process is completed by the application of a transparent glaze. The Staffordshire *sgraffiato* wares may be divided into two groups according to the character of their body. To the earlier group belong a jug and a mug in the Fitzwilliam Museum dated 1726 (1) and 1727 and decorated

---

(1) *Plate* 26.

respectively with figures of a stag and a hare drawn crudely but with much spirit; they are certainly the work of a single hand, and have the characteristic 'chamois-leather' body of the majority of the slip-painted dishes already described; for these a Staffordshire origin is probable, although it has been suggested that they may have come from potteries at Bolsover in Derbyshire, where slip ware of somewhat similar materials was made. In these two pieces the body has been covered with a thick coat of dark brown slip through which the decoration is cut; the glaze is deep yellow. Similar in technique is a posset-pot in the Hanley Museum, with a sucking-spout on one side and the date 1723, interrupted by a handsome floral design, on the other. The *sgraffiato* wares of the later group are more refined in shape and finish; their body is sometimes dark red (1), but in many cases it is in the nature of what came to be known as agate ware, from its likeness to the marking of that stone; it is produced by slicing finely and then mingling clays of different colours, light and dark. The glaze is of a pale cream colour. An exceptional piece, a small bowl, with a dark red body fired to the hardness of stoneware, has led to the association, almost certainly mistaken,[1] of this group of ware with a patent for a certain kind of salt-glazed ware granted in 1733 to Ralph Shaw of Burslem. Somewhat similar to this bowl in character is a larger basin in the Victoria and Albert Museum which is among the most striking of its kind; the outside is plain, but the *sgraffiato* design inside displays, below a chequer border, lions, fishes and sprays of flowers surrounding another lion in the middle (2). It is virtually certain (allowing for inaccuracies) that this bowl, which came from the Enoch Wood Collection, is the one described by Simeon Shaw on p. 109 of his *History*. Among the most pleasing examples of this later group are several jugs decorated with stripes of varying width traversed or interrupted by horizontal lines (3); a late jug, dated 1779, at Cambridge, has lines of beading done with a 'runner' before the scratching of the sprays of formal flowers which are the chief decoration. A dish with a rough bird design, dated 1753, in the Northampton Museum, and a loving-cup with leafy sprays in panelled zones, dated 1764, at Cambridge, have in common the use of painting in a cloudy slate blue under the glaze. A jug of excellent workmanship in the Hanley Museum, in a dark mahogany-red agate ware, is in a class by itself. On its shoulder is applied an oblong pad of white clay on which the word ALE is written in dark brown slip, as on a decanter label; a

[1] See W. B. Honey, 'English saltglazed stoneware', *Transactions of the English Ceramic Circle*, No. 1, 1933, p. 18.

(1) *Plate* 27; (2) *Plate* 28; (3) *Plate* 29

chain as if to suspend it is rendered in white slip round the neck. From its shape this jug should date from about 1760.

A small group of wares which may be mentioned here consists of those with glaze showing the purplish-brown mottle which perhaps denotes the presence of manganese, an ingredient mentioned in a passage of somewhat uncertain significance by Dr. Plot; as a rule they are devoid of decoration. A purplish-glazed wine-bottle or decanter of this class, of a shape well known in blue-and-white Lambeth delft ware, in the Victoria and Albert Museum, is painted with the cipher of Charles II in dark brown slip under the glaze; thus it belongs to the period of Dr. Plot's investigations.

The production of slip ware may have continued in minor pot-works in Staffordshire until late in the eighteenth century. Two dishes with a crudely drawn owl in the 'Toft' technique, formerly in the Lomax Collection, are dated 1772 and 1773 respectively. It is possible that they came from other small Midland potteries such as those of Bolsover and Ticknall in Derbyshire.

Taken as a class the Staffordshire slip wares constitute an achievement showing originality of invention and sometimes no small degree of aesthetic sensibility. The trailed slip technique was anticipated in a measure by London potters in the Middle Ages, and a jug found in Buckinghamshire, in the Victoria and Albert Museum,[1] is an interesting but rare example, probably of the sixteenth century, of applied relief ornament in white slip on a red 'body'; but there is no evidence to suggest that the men of Burslem were aware of any antecedents; they seem to have been prompted only by observation of the chromatic effects to be got by taking advantage of the variety of clays to hand in their own immediate neighbourhood. For the pictorial designs on their more ambitious wares they were no doubt indebted partly to the arts of the herald and the sign-painter, sometimes perhaps to engravings in books, but even in this field they were often obviously following their own fancy, in devising floral and animal themes which, though sometimes crude, are full of vitality and denote a nice sense of adaptation to the space available; this can be said not least of some of the wares in which the slip is trailed over a moulded relief outline. Fine examples are the early stag plate in the Fitz-william Museum and the later dishes with symmetrical bird and tree designs, in one case combined with 'sunface' flowers; these latter, attributable as we have seen to Samuel Malkin, are both represented in the British Museum. Designs in which the varied colouring attainable has been fully exploited are more obviously effective, but inven-

[1] Reproduced by B. Rackham, *Medieval English Pottery*, London, 1948, plate 91.

tion combined with skill in execution is most impressively shown in some cases where only two colours are present, a white slip on a red or dark brown ground; a dish in the Northampton Museum with a stylized tulip and leaves takes a high place for perfect distribution of ornament and steadiness of hand in its application (1).

---

(1) *Plate* 8.

3

ORIENTAL INFLUENCES:
THE BROTHERS ELERS AND THEIR
FOLLOWERS

While the slip ware potters were busy with their best achievements two events took place which were the prelude to what was no less than a revolution in their industry. The opening of trade with China by the various India Companies introduced tea to Western Europe and led to a steady change in drinking habits; a demand grew up for pottery of greater refinement than anything that had been made in England before. This was at first met by shipping from China—with the tea itself—the small red stoneware teapots made near Nanking which were used by preference in that country for serving the beverage. The second occurrence was the dynastic change by which the last Stuart king was obliged to quit the country and give up the throne to his daughter and her husband, William of Orange. Among the many personages who came over from Holland in the train of the new sovereigns were two silversmiths, the brothers John Philip and David Elers, who had conceived the idea of manufacturing in England teapots and other articles in fine pottery, to compete with those coming from China. According to the statement of one of them in a lawsuit, they had learnt how to make stoneware at Cologne and began to practise at Fulham in 1690; they had been cited with a number of other manufacturers as defendants for infringement of patents granted by Charles II to another potter working at Fulham who is now famous, John Dwight.

After a short period of production in that place the Elers brothers moved to Staffordshire and established themselves at Bradwell Wood, about two miles west of Burslem; here they continued to make fine red ware for some years by methods which as far as possible they kept secret, until about 1710. How long they remained in Staffordshire is uncertain—the elder brother was in Dublin as a china-merchant in 1700—and a contemporary record, in the diary of Lady Celia Fiennes, in 1698, implies that they had then ceased production in the district owing to the exhaustion of their local supply of suitable clay. There is less doubt as to the wares they made. A fair number of pieces survive, in hard unglazed ware ranging in colour from brick red to chocolate brown, which on chronological grounds could be attributed to them, but the difficulty is to distinguish their productions from the 'opacous red and dark-coloured porcelain or china' for which Dwight obtained a patent in 1684; nor is it possible to surmise which of the pieces that may be conjecturally accepted as their work were made at Fulham and which after their removal northward. A division by material is not practicable, since Dwight and presumably also the Elers brothers obtained clay from Staffordshire for the wares they made at Fulham. The fragments found by excavation in Bradwell Wood included both light red and dark. The whole question has been fully discussed by Mr. Honey in a paper read before the English Ceramic Circle.[1]

Among pieces that may with good reason be classed as Elers ware are a red teapot in the Victoria and Albert Museum with sprays of Chinese prunus blossom stamped by means of metal dies, and a mug in the Fitzwilliam Museum similarly ornamented with sprays, snails and a dancing merryandrew (1); the former has an impressed mark under its base, a stag in a circle, in the manner of those used by Dutch potters who made teapots of similar ware at Delft. Two pretty square bottles moulded with reliefs of Chinese figures and mounted with silver stoppers, one in the Victoria and Albert Museum, the other in the Cecil Higgins Museum, Bedford (2), may also reasonably be accepted as examples of Elers ware; Mr. Honey has plausibly argued that they were intended to contain tea rather than scent. These various articles herald the first arrival in Staffordshire of *chinoiserie*, which henceforward lasted in favour with the potters of the district alongside themes of native derivation and has survived in the blue-printed willow-pattern of the present day.

There was a revival of unglazed red ware of the Elers type towards the middle of the eighteenth century; the 'body' was eventually developed by Wedgwood and dignified with the name of *rosso antico*. These later wares have been the cause of much misunderstanding as to what the silversmith potters actually made. The motives of decoration on some of the pieces in this group show the impossibility of the classification formerly current. Such are the figure of Britannia, on a coffee-pot at Cambridge, with a shield marked 45 in allusion to the John Wilkes agitation in 1763 and the offending number of the *North Briton* newspaper; the king and queen joining hands below the initials GR and attended by two cupids, on two teapots of which one

[1] *Transactions* No. 2, 1934, p. 7 ff.

(1) *Plate* 30A; (2) *Plate* 30C.

has crabstock handle and spout, in the Victoria and Albert Museum, can only be George III and Charlotte, who were married in 1761. Some pieces of this class with 'rose-engine-turning' of the kind employed by Wedgwood are stamped underneath with the mark (ASTBURY) of a descendant of that Astbury of Shelton of whom more will be said below; some wares of this class are marked with an imitation Chinese seal in which a W is included, and these are almost certainly productions of Wedgwood himself, made in the early years of his career as a master-potter at Burslem.[1]

The innovations which the brothers Elers introduced into the Staffordshire potteries were twofold. It was doubtless their experience as silversmiths which suggested to them the use of a horizontal lathe to give their wares by turning, when hardened by drying, a smoother and more even surface than could easily be obtained in the process of throwing on the wheel. Their second novelty was decoration by means of small metal stamps or seals, with a pattern cut in intaglio, to produce the neat reliefs of foliage and other ornament found on the wares attributed to them; in this they were perhaps anticipated by Dwight, and something of the kind, but much less refined, had been done, as we have seen, by the slip ware potters with the help of stamps made of wood or baked clay. Lastly, following the Chinese, they provided against porosity not by applying a glaze but by hard firing. The result was the production of articles suitable for a tea-party, of a kind never seen in England before the importation from China began. It should be mentioned here that certain neatly-turned cups and mugs of red ware of the Elers type (1), formerly attributed to the brother potters, cannot be accepted as their work; the reliefs stamped on such pieces are similar to those on saltglaze ware of a kind made much later—about 1740 (see p. 22 below).

The new manufacture was a challenge to the native potters to improve their methods, and it was not long before they began to compete for the newly established trade. How they obtained their knowledge is a matter of conjecture or legend; that they got it surreptitiously is likely, but there are inherent inconsistencies in the story related by Simeon Shaw which need not be repeated here. The names of two local men, Astbury (whose Christian name is uncertain) and Joshua Twyford, are mentioned as pioneers in the exploitation of the new technique. Whether they were alone in the enterprise may be doubted; the fact remains that digging on the site of the factories of both men, situated within a short distance of one another near

[1] See W. B. Honey, *Wedgwood Ware*, London, 1948, pl. 14.

---

(1) *Plate* 30B.

Shelton Church, has yielded potsherds of ware precisely similar to that which it has long been customary to classify as 'Astbury ware'.

It has to be pointed out that there seems to be a considerable gap between the time of activity of the Elers brothers and the earliest date to which the tea and coffee services of what we may perhaps continue to call 'Astbury ware' were made, as will presently be seen. These services show a technical innovation which differentiates them from the unglazed ware of the 'Elers' type and from the earlier slip ware: they were submitted to two firings. Having first received the stamped reliefs with which they are usually ornamented, they were fired, like Elers ware, to what is known as the 'biscuit' condition; a red teacup and saucer with white reliefs, in the Victoria and Albert Museum, have never been carried beyond this stage. As a rule the wares were covered with a lead glaze which needed a second firing in what is called in Staffordshire a 'glost oven'. When thus fixed on the ware the glaze assumed a pale cream-coloured tone where seen over the white clay reliefs and gave a warm brownish gloss to the red 'body'. The decorations were not impressed directly on to the surface, as in the case of Elers ware, but upon pads of white pipeclay previously applied to receive them; they were apt to break or come out ragged if care was not taken in lifting the stamp or oiling it before use. In spite of these defects the earlier pieces so decorated are pretty, with little reliefs of interlaced scrollwork, tiny rosettes and leaves, and occasionally the Royal shield with lion and unicorn supporters (1). Evidence for the dating of these can be obtained by comparison with the white or drab saltglaze ware presently to be described, for decorating which identical stamps were often used. A date about the fourth decade of the eighteenth century seems most probable. Specimens are known in which clays firing to buff or deep brown have been used instead of red for lead-glazed wares otherwise of precisely the same character.

It is necessary to emphasize the fact that wares of this kind were made not only by Astbury and Twyford but also by other potters of the district. This is proved by the finding of wasters identical in type—showing, for instance, similar renderings of the Royal arms—on the site, at Little Fenton, of the factory of Thomas Whieldon, whose productions will be more fully treated on a later page. The essentials of 'Astbury' technique are continued, with an increase of competence and elaboration, in other lead-glazed wares to which it will be convenient to return when 'Whieldon ware' is discussed at length.

---

(1) *Plate* 31A, B. Finds at Fenton support the attribution of the jar to Whieldon.

4
STONEWARE. SALTGLAZE

Stoneware may be described as hard pottery fired to such a high degree of heat that the particles of the clay are fused into a semi-vitreous mass which is impervious to liquids and will withstand acids. Wares which can be classed under this name have been made in many different times and places; drainpipes and ginger-beer bottles provide examples in the present day. In Germany in the fifteenth century it was discovered that stoneware could be glazed by the volatilization of salt introduced into the kiln when a certain temperature has been reached; ware of this kind was found suitable for vessels to contain wine or beer. From the time of Queen Elizabeth onwards Rhenish wine was largely imported in stoneware bottles made chiefly in the neighbourhood of Cologne, and in the seventeenth century similar bottles, often difficult to distinguish from those which came from Germany, began to be made in London. John Dwight obtained from Charles II patents for making this and other kinds of stoneware in his pottery at Fulham; in 1693, as already mentioned, he opened legal proceedings against a number of potters for infringing his patent. Among the defendants were three potters of Burslem, Aaron, Richard and Thomas Wedgwood, kinsmen of him who was to make famous their family name.

In the records of these suits we have thus proof that before 1700 stoneware of the kind made later on a more extensive scale in the London district and elsewhere was being manufactured in Staffordshire. This documentary evidence lends support to the statement of Simeon Shaw that 'a rude kind of white stoneware' was made about 1685 by Thomas Miles of Shelton, from whitish clay mixed with fine sand from Baddeley Edge (two miles east of Burslem) and that another potter of the same name, at Hanley, made brown stoneware by mixing the same kind of sand with 'can marl' from the coal pits. These written records find confirmation in the discovery, in 1929, of wasters and fragments below the surface soil in the yard of the George Inn, Burslem; they are of coarse salt-glazed stoneware, grey in fracture, like that of Fulham and Lambeth, covered wholly or in part with a dressing of ferruginous brown clay. Several are of cylindrical mugs, reeded near the top and impressed with a small stamp showing

19

the crowned cipher of Queen Anne, as a certificate of capacity.[1] A few are ornamented with small applied medallions bearing a bust portrait of the queen in relief; they prove that a mug in the British Museum with rounded body and reeded neck and similar decoration—Queen Anne's head surrounded by three crowns—is of the same origin (1), although its sheeny russet-brown surface is surprisingly like that so characteristic of stoneware made throughout the eighteenth century at Nottingham. A small mug in the Victoria and Albert Museum, from the collection of the nineteenth-century potter Enoch Wood, can also be classed as a Staffordshire product of this period; a belt of reeding divides it into an upper deep brown zone and a lower buff, in the Lambeth and Fulham manner, but its waisted outline, with slightly rounded base, can be matched among the finds from the George Inn site in the Hanley Museum (2); it is interesting to note that there are mugs at South Kensington, also from the Wood Collection, of identical shape but in the usual buff earthenware of the slip-painted Stafford-shire dishes already described, with spotted brown glaze. In this con-nection, we find that 'stone ware and freckled' are said to have been made about 1710–15 by two Burslem potters, Thomas Taylor and Moses Shaw, in the memorandum of Josiah Wedgwood already cited.

In relating the origin of salt-glazing Simeon Shaw makes mention of 'Crouch ware' as having been first made at Burslem in 1690. For this he says that 'Common Brick Clay, and fine Sand from Mole cob were first used; but afterwards the Can Marl and Sand, and some persons used the dark grey clay from the coal pits and sand, for the body'; he adds that some potters mixed a proportion of red lead to the salt for glazing. The meaning of Crouch ware has been disputed. Earlier authorities thought it could be recognized in certain fine drab wares resembling in every respect except colour some of the white saltglaze ware to be described below; Mr. Honey, pointing out the impossibility that any such could be so early as the date given by Shaw, has con-vincingly suggested that the term relates to heavy stonewares such as those from the Wood Collection and the George Inn site. He has further conjectured that the word may be a corruption of the name of Crich, in Derbyshire, where brown stoneware is known to have been

[1] This stamp and similar ones with the cipher of William III can only be taken as evidence of the *earliest* possible date. Both appear to have lasted long in use by the Excise officers, since they are found on mugs which bear, *incised before firing*, dates long after the death of Queen Anne; for instance, a tankard in the Guildford Museum stamped WR has a relief bust of Queen Anne and, impressed with printer's type, the name of Adam Arnold of Ewell and the date 1765.

(1) *Plate* 33; (2) *Plate* 32A.

made with the bronze-like sheen characteristic of Nottingham ware
and found equally on some wares from Staffordshire.

From the evidence set forth above it seems clear that salt-glazed
stoneware was being made in Staffordshire from about 1685 onwards,
but that most of it was for the most ordinary uses and without
decoration of any kind; a small brown octagonal scent-bottle, formerly
in the Taylor Collection at Leicester, incised with the name and date
Anthony Bradley 1716, if of Staffordshire make, is an exceptional
piece. What is generally known as Staffordshire saltglaze is of a very
different character, and came into being when the 'body' made of
local clays was improved by mixing in it not only fine sand or ground
calcined flints but also a white pipeclay from Devon or Dorset. This
fine clay was brought by sea to Chester or the Mersey and thence by
packhorses to the Potteries in the form of balls of a size convenient for
handling; hence it is commonly known as 'ball clay'. Tradition gives
the credit for this improved body either to Astbury, the reputed
assistant of the brothers Elers, or to one Heath, of Shelton; however
this may be, the Staffordshire potters had been anticipated by Dwight
at Fulham, who made white stoneware by mixing calcined flint with
his clay, and it must be supposed that it was from him, through
channels of which we have no record, that they learned the secret.
The new body was used not only for salt-glazing but also, when fired
to a lower temperature, for lead-glazing by an improved method in
the manufacture of what came to be known as cream ware, of which
more will be said on a later page.

The impetus for developing a fine white-bodied ware suitable for
tea-table use came originally from China. Chinese porcelain was
imported in steadily increasing quantities during the seventeenth
century, and delft ware (buff earthenware coated with an opaque
white tin enamel) painted in blue or in several colours was made in
London and elsewhere to compete with it. Finally, from the first
decade of the eighteenth century, a new competitor entered the field
in the shape of porcelain made at Meissen and other places in Europe.
When white porcelain thus became readily purchasable, the red ware
made by the brothers Elers and those who adopted their methods fell
from favour and, if the now widespread fashion of tea-drinking was
to be accommodated, the Staffordshire potters found it imperative, if
they could not master the secrets of porcelain manufacture, to devise
another kind of ware which should possess the characteristic whiteness
of china. Efforts in this direction issued in the invention of white saltglaze ware, as described above. It seems that one of the chief pro-
ducers of this new ware was Dr. Thomas Wedgwood of Burslem, one
of the potters named in connection with Dwight's lawsuit.

From dated specimens which survive it appears that white salt-glaze was not made before the third decade of the eighteenth century; the biggest output was from about 1740 to 1760. The earliest dated example on record is a loving-cup incised with the date 1720, sold in London in 1934; next come a miniature circular pocket flask in the British Museum with, on one side, the initials and date I M 1724, and on the other a bird and branches incised and inlaid with brown clay (1), and a square scent-bottle moulded with *chinoiseries* in relief, in the Fitzwilliam Museum; the latter has scratched under its base the same date and initials T W which might possibly be those of Dr. Wedgwood. Few other pieces seem to remain from this early period. A plain white two-handled loving-cup incised with the names and initials of Martha Barbar and Cornelius Toft and the date 1727/8 is in the Northampton Museum; another loving-cup with brown inlaid date 1735 and rouletted mouldings, and a Nottingham stoneware cup with incised decoration dated 1740 indicate the probable age that can be assigned to such pieces as two teapots (in the Fitzwilliam and Victoria and Albert Museums) with incised trelliswork bands, their handle and spout being pressed in identical moulds. There are also a few pieces with ornaments stamped in the same manner as those in white on the red 'Astbury' wares, sometimes indeed with identical patterns, showing that they probably came from the same workshop (2). An unusual piece is a neat little teapot at Cambridge which has been carved into facets each stamped with a tiny spray or leaf (3). A dated piece (1750) in the British Museum, a small posset-cup (4) incised with the name of Mary Cowdale of Frolsworth, near Lutterworth, is exceptional in its lack of decoration of any kind, giving full effect to the fine quality of the ware.

An ingenious use of the stamping technique was on wares commemorating one of the many national triumphs of the period—the capture of Portobello (Panama) by Admiral Vernon in 1739 (5); small dies were cut in the shape of the admiral's figure, several small ships, the beleaguered forts, and strips of inscription recording the event; impressions of these were suitably assembled to portray the victory on the sides of a mug or sugar-basin.

A development of this method was the process generally known in the Potteries as 'sprigging'. The separate reliefs, instead of being stamped directly on to the surface of the ware, are made in small pads of clay pressed into intaglio moulds and then attached with liquid slip ('luted') to the surface (6). The results of this method, still practised

---

(1) *Plate* 34B; (2) *Plate* 39A; (3) *Plate* 39B; (4) *Plate* 52A; (5) *Plate* 36; (6) *Plate* 38A.

to-day, are familiar to everyone in the blue jasper ware of Wedgwood. Scroll and lacework ornaments and a tiny figure of Bacchus among vine branches may be mentioned among the decorations rendered with wonderful delicacy by this means; Chinese influence is unmistakable in sprays of prunus blossom with somewhat incongruous tendrils. The method was also employed for rendering vine stems in relief, the moulds being used for leaves, bunches of grapes, and flowers; thin threads of clay were rolled out between the palms of the hands, twisted into coils, and stuck on to the surface to form the stems of the vine. This procedure was anticipated exactly by German stoneware potters at Cologne for decorating their jugs in the sixteenth century. In teapots and other vessels thus decorated the handle and spout are of the kind called 'crabstock', made by moulding to imitate a gnarled branch, with stumps of small twigs often worked up afterwards with a tool; the vine stem is then applied as if springing from the base or top of the handle. We have here the explanation of the phrase 'handleing and vineing' which is found in an account-book of Thomas Whieldon (of whom more will be said) for the year 1749. Teapots of this class were made both in earthenware and in saltglaze ware, and in the latter case the body was usually thrown in the clay firing to a drab colour which, as mentioned already, was formerly associated with the term 'Crouch ware'; in this case the spout, handle and applied vine are in white clay. The agreeable contrast thus provided is perhaps seen at its best in drab stoneware decorated by stamping with the small lacework scrolls and the ornaments familiar on the so-called 'Astbury' red earthenware (1). A drab crabstock teapot of this kind, in the Hanley Museum, is reputed to have been made by Dr. Thomas Wedgwood, who died in 1737; if this tradition can be accepted, it takes back the manufacture of saltglaze ware of this description a few years earlier than the date provided by the Portobello commemorative pieces.

All these early pieces (except the flasks) are thrown on the wheel and subsequently turned. From about 1740 new methods came into use. Small trays and dishes, triangular, heart-shaped, star- or shell-shaped, or oblong with regular wavy sides (2), were made by pressing a 'bat' of clay into an intaglio mould made either of brass or alabaster. Similar moulds in two or three sections were used for 'hollow wares' (3), but for these a process which was of recent invention, that of casting, was introduced as it seems from France. Impressions from moulds, with or without intaglio patterns, are taken, and these when assembled, stuck together with slip and fired (usually also salt-glazed),

---

(1) *Plate* 38; (2) *Plates* 41A, 52B; (3) *Plate* 42C.

form a solid proof or 'block' (1); from this an unlimited number of working moulds can be taken as required, either in soft clay or in plaster of Paris, from which the actual pieces can be made by casting. The casting is done by uniting and tying together the constituent moulds and then pouring into them clay in a liquid slip from which the water is rapidly absorbed into the porous mould; slip repeatedly poured in until the clay lining formed inside the mould is sufficiently thick; the redundant liquid is then poured away, the mould left to dry, and then, its parts being separated, the vessel itself is released in readiness for firing. The process is equally suitable for earthenware or stoneware, for lead- or salt-glazing respectively.

By this process, brought to Staffordshire about 1745, table wares were made—teapots, coffee-pots, cups, cream-jugs, tea-caddies, basins, sauceboats and tureens, as well as mugs and flower-holders (to hang on a wall)—with decoration in slight relief which was sometimes picked out with japan gilding. The designs show surprising variety and inventiveness. Sometimes they are based on shells (2), wickerwork or floral compositions; in other cases they show little panels with figure-subjects mostly intentionally grotesque in character (3): books of travel, fables, or an engraving by Hogarth, have supplied the theme. Heraldry, cupids, small animals and *chinoiseries* jostle one another in deliberate incongruity. Even the shapes, of teapots especially, with small regard for function, are pressed into the semblance of a mansion, or a recumbent camel (4), a squirrel or even a man-of-war; the horizontal section is sometimes heart- or lozenge-shaped (5), or oblong quatrefoil. The resultant forms cannot always be defended artistically, but of the earlier saltglaze wares, whether thrown on the wheel, moulded or cast, it can be said that they show an admirable neatness of finish, a pleasant texture, and thin walls comparable for lightness with the best Chinese porcelain of the time.

Moulded saltglaze continued to be made for about twenty years after 1750, with steady deterioration of quality. A favourite type of decoration consists of basketwork and trellis of varying pattern in compartments separated by scrollwork with a slight rococo flavour; the trelliswork is sometimes perforated, as on the rims of dishes or plates or the lids of butter-dishes. 'Blocks' for making moulds with these and other patterns were made by Ralph Wood and his younger brother Aaron, of Burslem, of whom the former is well known as the first of two generations who specialized in the manufacture of earthenware figures; some of these blocks exist which are incised with the initials

---

(1) *Plates* 41B, 43A; (2) *Plates* 40B, 41B; (3) *Plates* 43, 37 A, B; (4) *Plate* 40A; (5) *Plate* 43C.

RW and dates ranging from 1749 to 1770 (1). The initials on the blocks may perhaps be no more than a mark of ownership, but that they indicate their maker may be argued on the analogy of the signature, incised on a block for a spittoon in the British Museum, of Aaron Wood, whose reputation as a block-cutter is on record. According to an inscription written on the back by his son Enoch, a large dish in the Victoria and Albert Museum was made by Aaron Wood about 1760. To this period approximately may be assigned plates with a border of trellis diaper in relief on the rim interrupted by a panel with the words: SUCCESS TO THE KING OF PRUSSIA AND HIS FORCES; over the diaper are imposed a bust of Frederick the Great and an eagle. Such plates, dating from the time of the king's popularity as an ally of the British Crown after the victories in the Seven Years War, were made both in saltglaze and in what is known as 'Whieldon ware'; the same holds good of some pieces for which the 'blocks' are preserved in the Wedgwood Museum at Etruria, and there is no doubt that these were made by Josiah Wedgwood during his early partnership with Whieldon at Fenton Low, and later, when he had a factory of his own at Burslem. Among them are a teapot, from a model said to be the work of William Greatbach, having on each side a relief of cattle in the foreground of a view of a mansion, also a cornucopia for flowers with a half-figure of Flora[1] and a sauceboat with scrolls and varied diapers.

Mention has been made of Aaron Wood, who was apprenticed in 1731 to Dr. Thomas Wedgwood and employed by several potters as a block-cutter. It was plausibly suggested by Frank Falkner that he was the author of a number of saltglaze figures and groups which, for all their *naïveté*, are among the most amusing and original creations of the Staffordshire potters of this period. Many of them belong to the class to which the name 'pew group' has become attached by collectors —very absurdly, because some include a wine-bottle and other accessories quite foreign to an ecclesiastical environment (2). The groups consist of three, or more often two, persons, a man and woman ogling one another, or musicians with fiddle or bassoon, sitting on a bench of which the high back is usually decorated, with heart-shaped perforations or a formal tree inlaid in dark brown, or small stamped leaves and flowers; features and details of costume (wig and frock coat or crinoline) are also rendered in dark brown. In one instance the bench has three giant masks applied in relief, done with a mould which, as Mr. Honey has observed, was also used to decorate some of the table ware. In the British Museum there is a saltcellar, with a date

---

[1] Reproduced by W. B. Honey, *Wedgwood Ware*, London, 1948, Plates 3, 13.

(1) *Plate* 41B; (2) *Plate* 46.

(1744) inlaid under its base, crudely but with much character modelled in the shape of a head (1); brown dots represent the eyes, and the hair is done with small coils of clay exactly like those of the wigs in some of the pew groups, thus providing an approximate date for these groups, which are evidently the work of a single individual, perhaps Aaron Wood. A unique model of the Fall, in the Fitzwilliam Museum, is also by this hand (2). The technique in all these is modelling by hand, with only the most sparing use of stamps or moulds for minor details; coats or skirts, aprons and stomachers, are made of thin slabs of clay folded and bent into the required shape, varied sometimes with overlaid strips of dark brown. The creation of these groups seems to be due to the wit and manipulative skill of their maker, unconscious of promptings from elsewhere; indeed, they anticipate by a little the earliest china figures made in England, and date from a time when even the Meissen porcelain figures which were to have such an extensive influence in this country were only at the beginning of their fashionable vogue.

Mention may be made here of jugs made in the shape of an owl (3) or bear (the latter usually hugging a terrier) (4), with head detachable to serve as a cup, which seem to have been very popular; they exhibit the same sense for the grotesque that is so evident in the pew groups. Details are picked out with spots or stripes of dark brown, and the fur of the bears is rendered by sprinkling with rough shreds of clay, a method sometimes used also in horizontal bands to vary the surface of teapots.

Similar in technique to the pew groups are a figure of a horseman (5) closely resembling several lead-glazed earthenware figures, such as the equestrian group to be described on p. 30, and a bell in the form of a comical figure of a woman. (6).

The pew groups and their like were soon to be followed by many other figures in saltglaze made by the same technique—pressing in moulds —as the china figures which, as time went on, they were obviously intended to emulate. The earlier are such as could be made very simply, by pressing in a two-piece mould (7); a figure in wig and gown, supposedly of Dr. Sacheverell is one of the most interesting models, and a pair of busts of the Empress Maria Theresa and her Consort cannot have been made before the election of Francis to the Imperial throne, in 1745. Several versions of a shepherd with dog, of which an example is known in unglazed red ware of the Elers type, are based on a small seventeenth-century bronze; another such bronze, taken in

---

(1) *Plate* 34A; (2) *Plate* 47; (3) *Plate* 50; (4) *Plate* 51A; (5) *Plate* 44; (6) *Plate* 35; (7) *Plates* 42 A, B; 45A, B.

its turn from the famed *Spinario* in Rome, must have been seen by the modeller of several neatly made figures of a boy drawing a thorn from his foot (1). A Chinese original has been used for figures of Shou Lao which, like the *Spinario*, are found also in earthenware with mottled lead glaze; a mould for such a Shou Lao dug up on the site of Whieldon's factory at Fenton makes it seem likely that many of these figures, salt-glazed or lead-glazed, were made at that place. Small saltglaze figures of birds, cats, pug dogs and other animals were very popular; they were moulded not only in plain white ware, with eyes and other details in brown or blue (2), but also in agate ware. Small objects such as scent-bottles were also made in salt-glazed agate ware (3), and the brown clay which is a constituent of this ware is used to coat the white 'body' of such rare pieces as a teapot at Cambridge, to set off applied stamped reliefs in white (4). From about 1755 the porcelain-maker's technique, of shaping in separate moulds and then assembling the several parts of a complicated figure, was adopted by the Staffordshire potters, and direct or indirect copies of the Meissen figures of birds, Italian Comedy actors, dancers and others became feasible and were produced (5).

Blue has been mentioned as used for details of saltglaze figures and this marks the introduction into Staffordshire of the employment of colours other than those afforded by the various types of clay. Cobalt was used with pretty effect in what is known as 'scratch blue' ware—white saltglaze in which an inscription or a floral or other design has been scratched with a pointed tool and then a clay slip or powder stained with cobalt has been rubbed into the incisions, before firing (6). The process was a favourite one for mugs and loving-cups made for individuals and bearing their names and a date. Dated examples range from 1724 to 1776 (7).

A large figure of Shakespeare in the Victoria and Albert Museum, based on the statue in Westminster Abbey by Scheemakers, is probably from the factory of Enoch Wood which was started in 1783; examples are common from the same model in earthenware with enamel painting. From this it is seen that saltglaze was still being made in Staffordshire late in the eighteenth century.

---

(1) *Plate* 48; (2) *Plate* 45B, 51B; (3) *Plate* 32B; (4) *Plate* 39A; (5) *Plate* 51; (6) *Plates* 43B, C, 53; (7) *Plates* 54, 55.

5

WHIELDON WARE

Concurrently with the saltglaze stoneware there was a steady production of lead-glazed earthenware. The two kinds of ware were often made in the same factory; the same 'body' was suitable for both. The same methods of throwing and turning, moulding or casting, were used for both, and for their decoration the same stamps and moulds did service. The difference was only in the clays used for the body and in the manner of firing and glazing; even for the body the same mixture of white-firing clay and ground flints employed for saltglaze was suitable, when fired to a lower degree of temperature, for whitish earthenware of the kind which came to be known as 'cream ware'. By adapting the methods of the old slip ware potters to the new conditions the makers of these finer wares were enabled for some time to hold their own. They relied on the attractiveness of colour, and sought steadily to widen the range available not only by the use of various clays in the 'body' and in ornamental accessories but also by the addition of staining oxides to their glaze materials. The lead was taken in these developments by Thomas Whieldon, who began potting at Little Fenton about 1740, and from this circumstance the term 'Whieldon ware' has become customary for the whole of this class of earthenware. The agate ware of the slip ware potters was improved upon. Some of the wares of this class dating from the early decades of the eighteenth century have great attractiveness owing solely to the beauty of colour of the mingled clays set off in shapes of austere simplicity (1). Variegation was sometimes increased by mixing manganese or cobalt with some of the clays which by fine slicing and blending produced a resemblance to the markings of natural stone, with more or less bizarre effect (2).

As a foil to the applied reliefs, whether of the small stamped ornaments of the 'Astbury' type or the 'sprigged' vine-stems already described which, if not invented, were at least extensively used by Whieldon, every shade of colour obtainable by a careful choice or blending of clay was brought into service, from pale buff to orange, red and dark brown. Crabstock handles and spouts were commonly

(1) *Plates* 56, 57; (2) *Plates* 58, 59.

B. TEAPOT AND MILK-JUG. EARTHENWARE WITH APPLIED RELIEFS.
H. (TEAPOT) 4¾ in. ABOUT 1740. *Victoria and Albert Museum. See page 29*

moulded in the same pale clay as the reliefs; teapots and milk-jugs were sometimes supported on three lion's-paw feet, in imitation of the silver plate by which many of the shapes in their entirety were inspired (1). A touch of manganese purple or blue, or at a later stage copper green, was sometimes added to the flowers and leaves of the reliefs to give greater diversity of colour (2). A hint was taken from the china-decorator and details were sometimes enriched with gilding—not yet the fluxed gold of modern usage but japanner's leaf gold, fixed with size and stoved. A shapely moulded teapot at Nottingham belonging to this period, inspired in its form by silversmith's work and moulded in relief with Chinese landscapes, is an unusual instance of the use of a dark red clay without further enhancement (3).

Whieldon's best achievement was undoubtedly the 'tortoiseshell' ware in which the manganese staining of the Queen Anne mottled wares was adapted to the almost colourless glaze now available, either alone or in combination with blue, yellow and green from oxides of cobalt, iron and copper. A masterpiece of the kind is a tureen in the Victoria and Albert Museum with applied leafy stems and a glaze 'clouded' with manganese purple alone (4). A dated example is a jug in the Hanley Museum with the date 1757 and the name Ralph Hammersley, said to be that of Whieldon's milkman. For these clouded and colour-glazed wares the improved white 'body' was employed already spoken of in describing saltglaze, in which calcined flint was mixed with local and Devon or Dorset clays. An improved method of preparing and applying the lead glaze, attributed to Enoch Booth of Tunstall was introduced about 1750. Instead of dusting the lead ore over the unfired ware he ground it up with flint and pipeclay and then mixed it with water to form a liquid into which the wares were dipped, but only after they had been fired to an absorbent biscuit condition; this necessitated a second firing in a 'glost' oven for fusing the glaze. This cream-coloured earthenware was later to be improved by Josiah Wedgwood into the Queen's ware, named in honour of Queen Charlotte, with which he established the supremacy of English pottery in the markets of the world.

Mention may here be made also of a tea-caddy dated 1779 as a late example showing the long continuance of glaze colouring of this order (5).

In 1754 Wedgwood, still a young man, was taken by Whieldon into partnership, and it was certainly his skill, enterprise and inventiveness which brought into being the later types of what is commonly classed

(1) *Colour Plate* B; *Plates* 61, 63A, B; (2) *Plates* 60, 63A, B; (3) *Plate* 62; (4) *Plate* 65; (5) *Plate* 64.

as Whieldon ware; as already pointed out, saltglaze ware was also part of the output of the partners, and many of the moulds they used served indifferently in the production of both kinds of ware. A green glaze derived from copper had been extensively used in the Middle Ages, but after the sixteenth century, for reasons which are not apparent, it fell into almost complete desuetude until it was taken up again by Wedgwood when working with Whieldon. To Wedgwood then are due the cauliflower and pineapple wares and the richer colourings of tortoiseshell ware distinguishable by their high standard of finish and workmanship. The later developments which resulted from this partnership and Wedgwood's subsequent career as an exponent in pottery of the Classical Revival are recounted in full by Mr. Honey in his book on Wedgwood.[1]

One class of lead-glazed ware made by Whieldon and many of his contemporaries from about 1750 onwards has a black body produced by mingling manganese with a dark-firing clay. The shapes in the earlier stages are those of the variegated and colour-glazed wares; decoration if used at all was by means of size gilding which has generally worn away with use. Exactly similar black ware was made at Jackfield in Shropshire, and where strong Staffordshire affinities or other clear evidences are wanting it is difficult to pronounce with confidence between the two possible sources.

As in saltglaze so also in lead-glazed ware a considerable production of figures began about the middle of the century. The earlier show all the characteristics as regards materials and colour of the so-called 'Astbury' table-wares; colouring of costume and other details was cleverly done by combining different kinds of clay, and the technique of modelling and eventually of pressing in moulds was the same as that followed for saltglaze figures. The earliest earthenware figures show a strong family likeness and are for the most part obviously the work of a single hand; Astbury is commonly and plausibly accepted as their author, but without evidence to prove the attribution. The range of subjects is wide, within the limits of what would be familiar in a country district; tradesmen, musicians, gamekeepers, troopers and infantry soldiers, ladies and milkmaids, and animals and birds, are rendered in a straightforward manner, seemingly in complete unconsciousness of the repertory of Court, theatrical and allegorical subjects which were favoured by the china factories; among the liveliest of all are the mounted figures, especially those of a man with his wife on a pillion (I).

[1] *Wedgwood Ware*, London, 1948.

(I) *Plates* 66, 69.

At a slightly later stage there is a change in technique and a widening of theme. Moulding became the method of shaping, and colour was obtained by enlisting the stained glazes which are associated with the name of Whieldon (I). Finds on the site of his factory have established that figures of this order were undoubtedly part of his output. At first the parti-coloured clay 'body' continued in combination with coloured glazes, but at last the colour was exclusively in the glazes, applied to a cream ware body. As with the saltglaze, the range of subjects was now widened; porcelain figures both Chinese and European, had come to the knowledge of the Staffordshire men, and tempted them to crude imitations which have only the attractiveness of their harmonious glaze colouring to recommend them. The most effective exploitation of the new techniques was in the hands of the Wood family and will be described on a later page.

(I) *Plates* 67, 68, 70, 71

6

PAINTED WARES: ENAMEL COLOURS AND BLUE-AND-WHITE

Competition with the attractiveness of porcelain was at last openly acknowledged when, according to Shaw, two Dutchmen set up enamelling ovens about 1750 at Cobridge (Hot Lane) for decorating saltglaze in bright colours in the manner of china. Their work was soon being imitated by enamellers brought, it is said, from London and Liverpool who, to begin with, carried on operations in the same neighbourhood. The wares decorated by these painters have in general a pleasing quality owing partly to the fact that the salt-glazed surface was peculiarly suitable for developing the pigments to a high degree of brilliance when fused in a muffle kiln. No signatures or marks were used, so that it is impossible to identify the work of individuals, but among the large quantity of surviving specimens certain hands can be distinguished by their style. It is conjectured that adaptations of Chinese themes—figures among flowering trees, or groups and sprays of more or less stylised flowers painted in jewel-like spots of vivid colour (1)—may be the work of the Dutchmen; to them is probably due the credit of enamelling some rare pieces closely imitating Japanese Kakiemon porcelain—unless perhaps these were among the wares sent 'in the white' to Holland to be decorated at Delft (2). Many pieces with a Jacobite reference can be attributed to these immigrant artists, such as a jug in the Harris Museum, Preston, with a figure of a highlander probably intended for Prince Charlie, and a tea-service of which the pieces are distributed in various collections (3). Among their presumed imitators one painted flowers in a bold summary manner in vivid colours (among which a clean turquoise blue is conspicuous) (4) and landscapes with figures that can be recognized by the heavy blue and purple clouds which often over-hang them and the feather-like treatment of foliage. He was the author of a jug in the British Museum inscribed 'Success to Mr. John Calverly of Leeds', a circumstance that suggests the possibility of his having been resident in that place, where in 1760 the firm of Robin-

---

(1) *Plate* 73; (2) *Plate* 72A; (3) *Plate* 72B; (4) *Plates* 74, 77.

son and Rhodes advertised themselves as enamellers of stoneware; against this possibility it has to be pointed out that the quantity of pieces painted by this enameller is surprisingly large for wares sent to a distance from their place of manufacture; moreover a jug decorated by the same hand and dated 1760, in the Hanley Museum (1), bears the portrait of an innkeeper at Checkley, near Uttoxeter, and is said to have been given to him by a clergyman who was partner of a Shelton potter and enameller, Warner Edwards; it is unlikely that this presentation piece would have been decorated outside the district. This enameller was master of many different styles, mostly derived directly or indirectly from Sèvres porcelain. The pastoral subject on one side of a handsome punch-pot with crabstock handle, in the Victoria and Albert Museum, is derived from Boucher. Recognizably by the same hand are pieces with a pink, turquoise or other coloured ground in the Sèvres manner and flowers or subject-panels in reserve; in a black and green diaper he is imitating Chinese *famille verte*. In some of his work a dark inky blue is characteristic. For panels with a portrait of Frederick the Great he uses a ground of royal ermine, and it is probable that a decoration can be attributed to him which is intended to imitate the fossils imbedded in natural stones, notably Derbyshire encrinite limestone (2).

Another saltglaze enameller whose work can be segregated painted Chinese flowers and figure subjects with sensitive wavering outlines (3); for his borders he often adopted trellis diapers of various patterns and differently coloured, edged with dainty black scrollwork. He seems also to have been responsible for the colouring of pieces with relief decoration such as teapots made to celebrate the wedding of George III in 1761. In general it may be said that the work of the saltglaze enamellers shows a wonderful variety of pleasing styles (4) and themes.

It is certain that saltglaze figures of the later sort—actors (5) and dancers and figures of swans and other birds, all of which are inspired in the last resort by originals in Meissen or Chinese porcelain—were sent 'in the white' to London to be coloured in his workshop at Kentish Town by the enameller William Duesbury, afterwards well known as the proprietor of the china factory in his native town of Derby. The British Museum possesses an account-book of Duesbury for the years 1751–3 in which 'swiming swans donn all over'[1] appear as an item,

[1] *William Duesbury's London Account Book*, with an introduction by Mrs. Donald MacAlister, London, 1931, p. 31.

(1) *Plate 75*; (2) *Plate 79*; (3) *Colour Plate C*; (4) *Plates 78, 80-83*; (5) *Plate 49*.

and precisely such figures of these and other birds exist completely covered with enamelling in the most brilliant colours, turquoise-blue, purple, orange-red, yellow and green, without any regard for their colouring in nature.

A number of teapots, sauceboats and other articles occur moulded with overlapping vine- or cabbage-leaves in a manner that was much in favour about the same period in the short-lived local porcelain-factory of William Littler, at Longton Hall; in some instances indeed identical moulds seem to have been used for saltglaze and porcelain, and in both we find a very similar use of enamelling to pick out the edges and veining of the leaves. Mention may be made here of another speciality reputed to have been devised by Littler; the white stoneware was dipped before firing in a clay slip stained with cobalt— the technique is parallel to that of the dark slip coating on the black ware of 'Jackfield' type. The result, after firing in the saltglaze kiln, was a rich blue surface approaching in colour the *bleu de roi* of Sèvres, sometimes left without further embellishment; most pieces however were afterwards painted with flowers and sprigs in opaque white and black enamels (1); the effect is pleasing, and recalls that of faïence made at Nevers and elsewhere in France in which the tin glaze is similarly stained blue as a ground for floral decoration in white and other colours. It was pointed out by Mr. William Burton that similar white enamelling on a blue ground occurs on porcelain believed to have been made at Longton Hall; size gilding, of which traces have sometimes escaped entire obliteration by wear, is also a feature common to both categories.

The Staffordshire potters cannot have been unacquainted with cobalt as a pigment for painting under or on the glaze in Chinese blue-and-white porcelain and in delft ware, but they were slow to include its use in their range of practice. They were at first precluded from doing so with success by their lack of a completely colourless lead glaze. On saltglaze ware it was employed, as we have seen, either as a stain or in the enameller's palette. A curious bowl in the British Museum dated 1743 has every appearance of being an experiment (2). It is painted in a slaty cobalt blue with designs in panels reserved on a ground mottled with manganese under a glaze of which the distinctly yellowish tone interferes greatly with the effectiveness of the painting. The themes chosen for painting are a curious blend of Chinese landscapes with deer and flowers on the outside and figures from the Old Testa- ment inside.

It was many years before the colourless glaze was evolved which was needful for developing a clean underglaze blue. A blue-and-white jug[1] with the name and date *Wm. Gallimore 1777* and emblems of farming is still of a deep cream colour. Two jugs in the Hanley Museum similarly painted, with Chinese buildings and trees, are dated respectively 1788 and 1790; the later (1) bears the name of Thomas Latham, of Chebsey, near Stafford. Rough but effective Chinese scenes of this kind in the manner of those on Lambeth delft are found on blue-and-white plates with shell edge stamped with the mark ASTBURY; they were probably made at Fenton by Joshua Astbury or his son Richard Meir (who directed the factory from about 1785 to 1800) whose initials RMA are stamped on the front of jugs moulded with a group of bird's-nesters.

The classical mode introduced into the Potteries by Wedgwood in the last quarter of the eighteenth century exercised a compelling influence on his rivals. Even the cream-coloured ware in which, in a modified form, the early traditions were carried on, was made—in Wedgwood's hands—to conform to the new discipline. In smaller factories the old fashions of shape and style endured for a while, and the technique of overglaze enamel painting introduced from abroad in the first instance for the decoration of white saltglaze was adapted to lead-glazed cream ware. The brilliant colours of enamelled saltglaze were unattainable, but a palette suitable to the yellowish tone was evolved which was employed for a variety of unpretentious but attractive themes. Names and dedicatory inscriptions are frequent, enclosed by feathery scrollwork in modest imitation of silversmith's and bookplate-engraver's art. A teapot in the Hanley Museum is painted with scrollwork of this kind and the legend 'Wilkes and Liberty', in reference to the political agitations of 1763 and afterwards. Dated examples show that this kind of thing continued into the last quarter of the eighteenth century. A bust of Queen Charlotte on one side of a teapot (indicating a date about the time of her marriage—1761) is companioned on the other by a rough village scene with a church among trees (2). Landscapes of this order were much in favour, sometimes with pavilions or palisades which betray Chinese influence (3). Bunches of flowers in gay red, green, purple and yellow sometimes occur, but a more restricted colour scheme is usual—black effectively combined with red or chocolate, or black or red alone (4). These decorations, though not unconscious of the fashions of the day, show a simplicity and originality of treatment, especially in choice of colours, which is not without merit. A jug with an inscription con-

[1] Formerly in a private collection at Buxton.

(1) *Plate* 85; (2) *Plate* 86; (3) *Plate* 88; (4) *Plates* 86, 87.

necting it with Betley, a few miles west of Burslem, and therefore almost certainly of Staffordshire make, has intertwined handles such as are usually associated with the Leeds pottery, where they were much in favour (1). Particularly effective are nondescript all-over patterns in the manner of chintz. At last gaiety of this kind was banished under the sobering influence of Wedgwood's classicism, to await a reawakening under the Regency in the nineteenth century.

---

(1) *Plate* 89.

D. 'TOBY JUG'. EARTHENWARE PAINTED IN COLOURED GLAZES.
H. 10 in. MADE AT BURSLEM BY RALPH WOOD THE ELDER FROM
A MODEL BY JOHN VOYEZ. ABOUT 1770.
Victoria and Albert Museum
See page 37

7

THE WOODS AND
THEIR CONTEMPORARIES

Even after Wedgwood had established the ascendancy of the Classical, embodied in the wide variety of new and improved wares invented by his genius, there was one class of production in which the earlier Staffordshire traditions of technique continued for some time to survive. As we have seen, both in saltglaze ware and in the lead-glazed earthenware associated with the names of Astbury and Whieldon there had been a lively output of figures which received a powerful impetus when china factories were started in England to compete with Meissen in this as well as other branches of production. A steady demand was thus created for figures in materials less costly to produce than porcelain. To meet this demand Ralph Wood of Burslem (1716–72), already mentioned as a saltglaze manufacturer, turned his attention especially to the production of coloured figures in great variety cheap enough to find a place in the homes of farmers and cottagers. His figures owe their attractiveness largely to the harmonious tones of metallic colours—cobalt blue, manganese purple, copper green and iron yellow, often supplemented with a deep brown clay slip applied on the white biscuit 'body' before dipping in the almost colourless transparent glaze which was now available (1). Ralph Wood's Toby jugs modelled after the engraved illustration of a ballad about a notorious Yorkshire toper are so well known that they may be cited as typical of the colouring of all his productions (2). It is fairly well established that although on its technical side the line taken by Wood's factory was dictated by his own skill and enterprise, he was indebted for most of his models to a French artist, John Voyez, who settled in Staffordshire; the signature of Voyez is found on a few pieces, notably impressed on some jugs moulded in the form of a treetrunk with bird's-nesters gathered round it and inscribed with an invocation to 'Fair Hebe'; the exactly similar jugs made in imitation of Wood's by R. M. Astbury have already been mentioned.[1] The

[1] p. 35.

(1) *Plates* 90, 91; (2) *Colour Plate* D.

repertory of subjects was now widened: rustic characters were driven into the background and the gods of Olympus were introduced to the countryside; the new evangelism created a market also for the Pauline virtues and for figures illustrating Bible stories (1), particularly those of the Old Testament. At the same time, for the less serious-minded, Wood made provision for the ribaldry of opposing schools of churchmanship: Hudibras on his horse after an engraving by Hogarth is countered by satirical groups of parson and clerk, either as the 'Vicar and Moses' in a double-decked pulpit or returning from an evening carouse. Among the most delightful of the models from his factory mention must be made of deer, foxes and other animals and birds for which his soft underglaze colours were admirably suited (2).

Ralph Wood was succeeded by his son of the same name (1748–97) who introduced two new techniques of colouring in the factory. One consists of the painting in underglaze pigments of a kind usually connected with Felix Pratt, a Fenton potter, who employed them on 'useful' wares marked with his name (3); the colours are akin to those of the older Wood, but include also brown, orange and green of a peculiar opaque quality due to blending of oxides and perhaps an admixture of clay slip. Colouring of this order is to be found both in figures and useful wares and in plaques with low reliefs (made for hanging on a wall) which now became popular. The younger Wood's second innovation was a concession to porcelain-painting; he introduced bright overglaze enamel colours requiring a third firing to fix them, of a tonality like those on Chelsea-Derby china (4). He was succeeded as manager by his cousin Enoch (1759–1840), son of the block-cutter Aaron Wood; the enamel-painted portrait busts and ambitious groups, often of large size, made under the new direction bring us into the history of Staffordshire in the nineteenth century. Before closing, a backward glance may be given to the excellent work of Henry Neale of Hanley and his partner (from 1786) and successor. David Wilson, in the last quarter of the eighteenth century (5). Much of his output was in emulation of the classical wares of Wedgwood, but he continued and refined the early figure-modelling tradition in a number of works, mostly of small dimensions, which are noteworthy both for their fine finish and restraint of colouring, and for the good judgment shown in modelling with a view to shaping in a mould which in most cases was in two parts only.

(1) *Plate* 91; (2) *Plates* 92, 93; (3) *Plate* 96; (4) *Plate* 94; (5) *Plate* 95 A–D.

BIBLIOGRAPHY AND INDEX

BIBLIOGRAPHY

The first literary evidences for the early history of the Staffordshire potteries are discussed in Chapter I. Information on the subject is given in many books dealing with English pottery in general. The subjoined list gives the more important of these, as well as documentary books dealing with particular aspects of the subject. Papers by various authors printed in the *Transactions of the English Ceramic Circle*, from 1933 onwards, embody the results of researches which are indispensable to a detailed study of the subject from a historical point of view.

BURTON, WILLIAM, *A history and description of English earthenware and stoneware*. London, 1904.

CHURCH, Sir ARTHUR, *English Earthenware*. 2nd edition. London, 1911.

FALKNER, FRANK, *The Wood Family of Burslem*. London, 1912.

HOBSON, R. L., *Catalogue of the Collection of English Pottery in the British Museum*. London, 1903.

HOBSON, R. L., *A Guide to the English Pottery and Porcelain in the British Museum*. 3rd edition. London, 1923.

HODGKIN, JOHN ELIOT, and EDITH, *Examples of early English Pottery, named, dated and inscribed*. London, 1891.

HONEY, W. B., *English Pottery and Porcelain*. London, 1949 (4th edition).

HONEY, W. B., *Wedgwood ware*. London, 1948 (The Faber Monographs on Pottery and Porcelain).

JEWITT, LLEWELLYN, *The Ceramic Art of Great Britain*. London, 1878.

LOMAX, CHARLES J., *Quaint old English Pottery*. Manchester, 1909.

RACKHAM, BERNARD, and READ, HERBERT, *English Pottery*. London, 1924.

RACKHAM, BERNARD, *Victoria and Albert Museum, Department of Ceramics, Catalogue of English porcelain, earthenware, enamels and glass collected by Charles Schreiber, Esq., M.P., and the Lady Charlotte Elizabeth Schreiber and presented to the Museum in 1884*. Vol. II. London, 1928.

BIBLIOGRAPHY

RACKHAM, BERNARD, *Catalogue of the Glaisher Collection of pottery and porcelain in the Fitzwilliam Museum, Cambridge*. Cambridge, 1935.

RHEAD, GEORGE WOOLLISCROFT and FRANK A., *Staffordshire Pots and Potters*. London, 1906.

SOLON, M. L., *The Art of the old English Potter*. London, 1883.

WEDGWOOD, JOSIAH CLEMENT, *Staffordshire Pottery and its History*. London, n.d.

INDEX

43

INDEX

PLATES

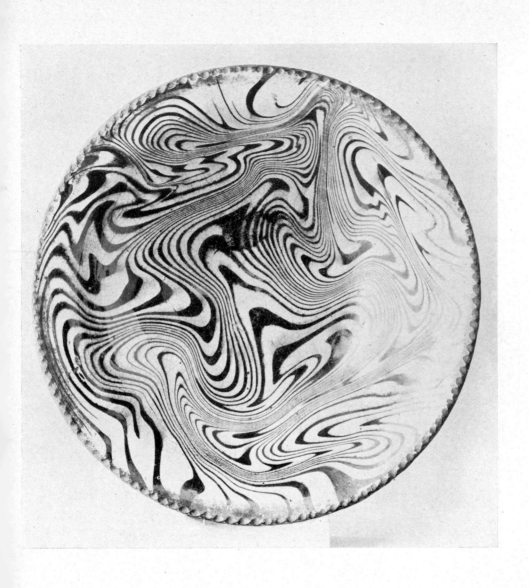

1. DISH. MARBLED SLIP WARE. DIAM. 13¾ in. LATE SEVEN-
TEENTH OR EARLY EIGHTEENTH CENTURY.
Victoria and Albert Museum
See page 7

2. DISH. SLIP WARE. DIAM. 18 in. ABOUT 1660-1680.
Victoria and Albert Museum
See page 6

3. DISH. SLIP WARE. DIAM. 17 in. ABOUT 1660-1680.
British Museum
See page 6

4. DISH. SLIP WARE. CHARLES II AND CATHERINE OF BRAGANZA.
DIAM. $17\frac{1}{4}$ in. ABOUT 1662-1670. *Cambridge, Fitzwilliam Museum*
See page 6

5. DISH. SLIP WARE. A KING, PROBABLY CHARLES II. DIAM.
17 in. ABOUT 1670-1680. *Cambridge, Fitzwilliam Museum*
See page 10

6. DISH. DECORATED IN WHITE, RED AND OLIVE-GREEN SLIPS
ON A DARK BROWN GROUND. DIAM. 22 in. ABOUT 1670-1680.
Cambridge, Fitzwilliam Museum
See pages 7, 10

7. POSSET-POT. SLIP WARE. INSCRIBED: *The best is not too good for you.* H. 9 in. DATED 1692. *Cambridge, Fitzwilliam Museum.*
See pages 8, 9

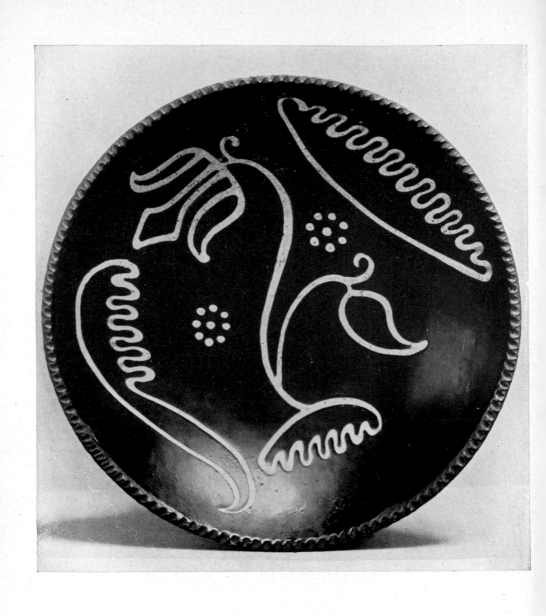

8. DISH. WHITE SLIP ON DARK BROWN GROUND. DIAM 13 in.
LATE SEVENTEENTH OR EARLY EIGHTEENTH CENTURY.
Northampton, Central Museum
See pages 6, 14

9A. JUG. WHITE SLIP ON DARK BROWN GROUND. H. $6\frac{1}{4}$ in.
PERHAPS MADE AT TICKENHALL, DERBYSHIRE. SEVENTEENTH
CENTURY. *Victoria and Albert Museum*
9B. PIGGIN. STAMPED DECORATION IN WHITE SLIP ON A DARK
BROWN GROUND. H. $3\frac{1}{4}$ in. LATE SEVENTEENTH OR EARLY
EIGHTEENTH CENTURY. *Cambridge, Fitzwilliam Museum*
See pages 6, 7

10. A. LOVING-CUP. H. 5 in.
B. BLEEDING-BOWL. DIAM. 5 in. SLIP WARE. LATE SEVENTEENTH
OR EARLY EIGHTEENTH CENTURY. *Cambridge, Fitzwilliam Museum*
See pages 6, 8

11. A. HONEY-POT. WHITE SLIP ON A DARK BROWN GROUND.
H. 5⅜ in. LATE SEVENTEENTH OR EARLY EIGHTEENTH CENTURY.
Mr A. J. B. Kiddell
B. CUP. DECORATED IN OLIVE-GREEN AND DARK BROWN SLIP.
INSCRIBED: *Beware wheresoere you be For from deceit no Place is
Free.* H. 4 in. LATE SEVENTEENTH CENTURY.
Cambridge, Fitzwilliam Museum
See pages 6, 7

12. DISH. WHITE SLIP ON RED GROUND. DIAM. $16\frac{1}{2}$ in. LATE
SEVENTEENTH OR EARLY EIGHTEENTH CENTURY.
Victoria and Albert Museum
See page 7

13. DISH. RED SLIP ON WHITE GROUND. DIAM. 19 in. DATED 1704.
British Museum
See page 7

14. MUG. SLIP WARE. H. 4 in. DATED 1694.
Cambridge, Fitzwilliam Museum
See page 7

15. MUG. SLIP WARE. H. $4\frac{3}{8}$ in. LATE SEVENTEENTH OR EARLY
EIGHTEENTH CENTURY. *Victoria and Albert Museum*
See page 7

16. OWL JUG, WITH HEAD DETACHABLE TO SERVE AS A CUP.
COMBED SLIP WARE. H. 8½ in. LATE SEVENTEENTH OR EARLY
EIGHTEENTH CENTURY. *British Museum*
See page 8

17. POSSET-POT. SLIP WARE. INSCRIBED: *Robbort Wood. The best is not too good for you.* H. 6¾ in. LATE SEVENTEENTH CENTURY
Stoke-on-Trent, Hanley Museum and Art Gallery
See page 9

18. POSSET-POT. SLIP WARE WITH MARBLED DECORATION. H.
5⅝ in. DATED 1682. *Victoria and Albert Museum*
See page 7

19. DISH. SLIP WARE. DIAM 13¾ in. LATE SEVENTEENTH OR EARLY EIGHTEENTH CENTURY. *Victoria and Albert Museum*
See page 6

20. PLATE. MOULDED SLIP WARE. DIAM. 9 in. MIDDLE OF
SEVENTEENTH CENTURY. *Cambridge, Fitzwilliam Museum*
See page 9

21. PLATE. MOULDED SLIP WARE. DIAM. $9\frac{1}{2}$ in. MIDDLE OF
SEVENTEENTH CENTURY. *Cambridge, Fitzwilliam Museum*
See page 8

22A. DISH. MOULDED SLIP WARE. DIAM 16¼ in. ABOUT 1751.
Manchester, City Art Gallery
See page 8
22B. JAR. SLIP WARE. H. 5⅛ in. ABOUT 1700.
Cambridge, Fitzwilliam Museum
See page 6

23A. MOULD FOR A DISH. SIGNED BY WILLIAM BIRD AND DATED
1751. DIAM. 13¾ in. *British Museum*
See page 8
23B. EGG-STAND. DIAM. 6¾ in. LATE SEVENTEENTH CENTURY.
Cambridge, Fitzwilliam Museum
See page 8

24. DISH. MOULDED SLIP WARE, WITH INITIALS OF SAMUEL
MALKIN. DIAM. 17 in. ABOUT 1710-1720.
Cambridge, Fitzwilliam Museum
See pages 9, 10

25. DISH. MOULDED SLIP WARE. INSCRIBED *RS* DIAM. $17\frac{1}{2}$ in.
FIRST HALF OF EIGHTEENTH CENTURY. *British Museum*
See page 9

26. JUG. SLIP WARE, WITH *sgraffiato* DECORATION. H. $5\frac{7}{8}$ in.
DATED 1726. *Cambridge, Fitzwilliam Museum*
See page 11

27. MUG. SLIP WARE, WITH *sgraffiato* DECORATION. H. $6\frac{1}{8}$ in.
DATED 1747. *Victoria and Albert Museum*
See page 12

28. BOWL. *Sgraffiato* WARE. DATED 1755. DIAM $5\frac{7}{8}$ in.
Victoria and Albert Museum
See page 12

29. JUG. *Sgraffiato* WARE. MIDDLE OF EIGHTEENTH CENTURY.
H. $5\frac{7}{8}$ in. *Northampton, Central Museum*
See page 12

30A. MUG. UNGLAZED RED WARE, WITH STAMPED DECORATION.
MADE BY THE BROTHERS ELERS. H. 4 in. LATE SEVENTEENTH
CENTURY. *Cambridge, Fitzwilliam Museum*

30B. COFFEE-CUP. UNGLAZED RED WARE, WITH STAMPED
DECORATION. H. $2\frac{3}{8}$ in. ABOUT 1740. *Victoria and Albert Museum*

30C. TEA-JAR OR SCENT-BOTTLE. UNGLAZED RED WARE,
MOULDED IN RELIEF. MADE BY THE BROTHERS ELERS. H. $5\frac{1}{8}$ in.
LATE SEVENTEENTH CENTURY. *Bedford, Cecil Higgins Museum*
See pages 16, 17

31A. JAR. GLAZED RED WARE WITH HANDLES IN WHITE CLAY.
H. 4 in. ABOUT 1740. *Cambridge, Fitzwilliam Museum*
See page 18

31B. TEAPOT. GLAZED RED WARE WITH APPLIED RELIEFS IN
WHITE. H. 4⅛ in. ABOUT 1740. *Victoria and Albert Museum.*
See page 18

32A. MUG. BROWN SALT-GLAZED STONEWARE. DUG UP AT THE
GEORGE INN, BURSLEM. H. $2\frac{5}{8}$ in. EARLY EIGHTEENTH CENTURY.
Stoke-on-Trent, Hanley Museum and Art Gallery
32B. SCENT-BOTTLE. SALTGLAZE AGATE WARE. DIAM. 1 in.
ABOUT 1745. *Cambridge, Fitzwilliam Museum*
See pages 20, 27

33. MUG. BROWN SALT-GLAZED STONEWARE, WITH APPLIED
BUST OF QUEEN ANNE. H. $4\frac{7}{8}$ in. EARLY EIGHTEENTH CENTURY.
British Museum
See page 20

34A. SALTCELLAR. WHITE SALTGLAZE WARE, WITH INCISED
INITIALS FILLED IN WITH BROWN SLIP. H. 3 in. DATED 1744.
British Museum
See page 26
34B. FLASK. WHITE SALTGLAZE WARE, WITH INCISED DECORA-
TION FILLED IN WITH BROWN SLIP. H. $3\frac{1}{2}$ in. DATED 1724.
British Museum
See page 22

35. BELL. WHITE SALTGLAZE WARE. H. 5¾ in. ABOUT 1740.
Victoria and Albert Museum
See page 26

36. MUG. WHITE SALTGLAZE WARE, WITH APPLIED RELIEFS
COMMEMORATING THE CAPTURE OF PORTOBELLO. H. 6⅞ in.
ABOUT 1740. *Victoria and Albert Museum*
See page 22

37. MILK-JUG. WHITE SALTGLAZE WARE, CAST, WITH RELIEF
DECORATION. H. 6½ in. ABOUT 1745. *Victoria and Albert Museum*
See page 24

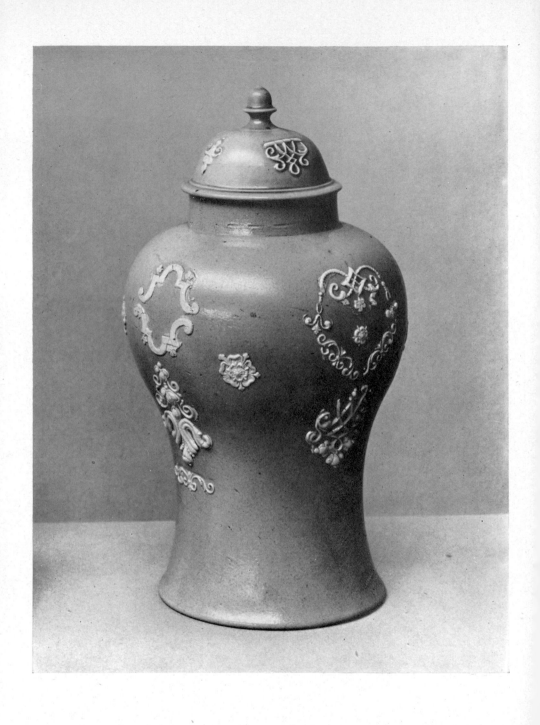

38. MUG. DRAB SALTGLAZE WARE, WITH APPLIED RELIEFS IN
WHITE. H. 5¼ in. ABOUT 1745. *Victoria and Albert Museum*
See pages 22, 23

39A. TEAPOT. WHITE SALTGLAZE WARE COATED WITH BROWN
SLIP AND DECORATED WITH APPLIED RELIEFS OF THE ROYAL
ARMS IN WHITE. H. 4 in. ABOUT 1740.
Cambridge, Fitzwilliam Museum
See pages 22, 27

39B. TEAPOT. WHITE SALTGLAZE WARE, WITH CARVED AND
STAMPED DECORATION. ABOUT 1740. H. 3⅜ in
Cambridge, Fitzwilliam Museum
See page 22

40A. TEAPOT. H. 4½ in. ABOUT 1745
See page 24
40B. CREAM-JUG. CAST FROM THE BLOCK PLATE 41B. H. 3 in.
ABOUT 1750. BOTH WHITE SALTGLAZE WARE, CAST, WITH RELIEF
DECORATION TOUCHED WITH BLUE. *Victoria and Albert Museum*
See page 24

41. A. PICKLE-TRAY. PRESSED IN A MOULD. W. 6¼ in. ABOUT 1750.
41. B. BLOCK FOR A CREAM-JUG. MARKED WITH THE INITIALS OF
RALPH WOOD OF BURSLEM. H. 3½ in. DATED 1749. BOTH WHITE
SALTGLAZE WARE. *Victoria and Albert Museum*
See pages 23, 24, 25

42A. FIGURE. WHITE SALTGLAZE WARE, WITH IMPRESSED
ORNAMENTS. H. 3⅜ in. ABOUT 1745.
Cambridge, Fitzwilliam Museum
See page 26

42B. FIGURE. SALTGLAZE AGATE WARE, WITH IMPRESSED
DETAILS. H. 4½ in. *Cambridge, Fitzwilliam Museum*
See page 26

42C. TEA-CADDY. WHITE SALTGLAZE WARE, MOULDED WITH
TEA-PLANTS IN RELIEF, INSCRIBED *CIA or TE herb.* H. 3¾ in.
ABOUT 1750. *Victoria and Albert Museum*
See page 23

43A, B. TEA-CUP WITH RELIEF AND 'SCRATCH BLUE' DECORATION
(H. 2 in.) AND BLOCK FROM WHICH IT WAS CAST (H. 2½ in.).
WHITE SALTGLAZE WARE. ABOUT 1740.
Victoria and Albert Museum
43C. TEAPOT. WHITE SALTGLAZE WARE, CAST, WITH RELIEF
AND 'SCRATCH BLUE' DECORATION. H. 5½ in. ABOUT 1740.
Cambridge, Fitzwilliam Museum
See pages 24, 27

44. FIGURE OF A HORSEMAN. WHITE SALTGLAZE WARE WITH
DETAILS IN BROWN SLIP. H. 9¼ in. ABOUT 1745.
Victoria and Albert Museum
See page 26

45. A. FIGURE REPUTEDLY OF DR SACHEVERELL. WHITE SALT-
GLAZE WARE WITH DETAILS IN BROWN. H. 6 in.
45. B. GROUP, SALTGLAZE AGATE-WARE MOTTLED WITH BLUE. H.
3¼ in. BOTH ABOUT 1745. *Cambridge, Fitzwilliam Museum*
See pages 26, 27

46. GROUP. WHITE SALTGLAZE WARE WITH DECORATION INLAID
IN BROWN. H. 6¼ in. ABOUT 1745. *Cambridge, Fitzwilliam Museum*
See page 25

47. GROUP. THE FALL. WHITE SALTGLAZE WARE WITH DETAILS
IN BROWN. ABOUT 1745. *Cambridge, Fitzwilliam Museum*
See page 26

48. FIGURE. THE *Spinario*. WHITE SALTGLAZE WARE. H. 5¼ in.
ABOUT 1755. *Cambridge, Fitzwilliam Museum*
See page 27

49. PAIR OF FIGURES OF TURKS, AFTER MODELS IN MEISSEN
PORCELAIN BY JOHANN JOACHIM KÄNDLER. WHITE SALTGLAZE
WARE WITH ENAMEL PAINTING. H. 7¾ in. ABOUT 1755-60.
Victoria and Albert Museum
See pages 27, 33

50. JUG IN THE FORM OF AN OWL, WITH HEAD TO SERVE AS A CUP. WHITE SALTGLAZE WARE WITH DETAILS IN BROWN AND GREY SLIP. H. 8½ in. ABOUT 1740. *Cambridge, Fitzwilliam Museum*
See page 26

51A. JUG IN THE FORM OF A BEAR HUGGING A TERRIER, THE
HEAD SERVING AS A CUP. WHITE SALTGLAZE WARE WITH
DETAILS IN BROWN. H. 3¾ in. ABOUT 1740.
Victoria and Albert Museum
See page 26
51B. FIGURE OF A DOG. WHITE SALTGLAZE WARE WITH MARK-
INGS IN BLUE, BROWN EYES. H. 5⅝ in. ABOUT 1745.
Cambridge, Fitzwilliam Museum
See page 27

52A. POSSET-CUP. WHITE SALTGLAZE WARE. INCISED WITH
NAME AND DATE: *Mary Cowdal of Frolsworth* 1750. H. 4$\frac{3}{8}$ in.
British Museum
See page 22

52B. JELLY-MOULD. WHITE SALTGLAZE WARE. D. 3$\frac{3}{4}$ in. ABOUT
1750. *Victoria and Albert Museum*
See page 23

53. ALE-JUG. WHITE SALTGLAZE WARE, WITH 'SCRATCH BLUE'
DECORATION. INCISED UNDER THE BASE WITH NAME AND DATE:
I.B. 1751. H. 7 in. *Mr and Mrs J. E. Lowy*
See page 27

54. MUG. WHITE SALTGLAZE WARE, WITH 'SCRATCH BLUE'
DECORATION. INSCRIBED: 17 *Enoch Booth* 42. H. 4¾ in. DATED
1742. *Cambridge, Fitzwilliam Museum*
See page 27

55. MUG. WHITE SALTGLAZE WARE, WITH 'SCRATCH BLUE'
DECORATION. H. 5 in. DATED 1752. *Victoria and Albert Museum*
See page 27

56. MUG. AGATE WARE. H. $5\frac{1}{8}$ in. ABOUT 1740.
Northampton, Central Museum
See page 28

57. POSSET-POT. DARK RED EARTHENWARE WITH MARBLING in
WHITE. H. 6¾ in. ABOUT 1740. *Victoria and Albert Museum*
See page 28

58. SUGAR-BASIN. AGATE WARE. H. 4¾ in. ABOUT 1740.
Cambridge, Fitzwilliam Museum
See page 28

59. TEAPOT. AGATE WARE. H. 4 in. ABOUT 1740.
Victoria and Albert Museum
See page 28

60. TEAPOT. BUFF EARTHENWARE, WITH HANDLES AND SPOUT
IN WHITE AND APPLIED RELIEFS TOUCHED WITH SLATE-BLUE
PIGMENT. H. 3⅜ in. ABOUT 1740. *Victoria and Albert Museum*
See page 29

61. TEAPOT. DARK BROWN EARTHENWARE, WITH APPLIED RELIEFS
IN WHITE. H. 4¾ in. ABOUT 1750. *Victoria and Albert Museum*
See page 29

62. TEAPOT. GLAZED DARK RED EARTHENWARE, MOULDED IN
RELIEF. H. 6 in. ABOUT 1745. *Nottingham, Museum and Art Gallery*
See page 29

63A. TEAPOT. DARK BROWN EARTHENWARE, WITH VINE-STEMS
APPLIED IN RELIEF AND COLOURED DARK GREEN AND PURPLISH
BLUE. H. $3\frac{1}{2}$ in. ABOUT 1745. *Manchester, City Art Gallery*
See page 29
63B. MILK-JUG. DEEP OCHRE-COLOURED EARTHENWARE, WITH
HANDLES AND LIP IN WHITE AND APPLIED RELIEFS TOUCHED
WITH GREEN, MANGANESE-PURPLE AND BLUE. H. $4\frac{1}{2}$ in. ABOUT
1745. *Mr and Mrs T. M. Ragg*
See page 29

64. TEA-CADDY. CREAM-COLOURED WARE, WITH APPLIED
RELIEFS TOUCHED WITH UNDERGLAZE PIGMENTS. INCISED WITH
INITIALS AND DATE: *I. M.* 1779. H. 57 in.
Victoria and Albert Museum
See page 29

65. SOUP-TUREEN. 'TORTOISESHELL WARE', WITH APPLIED
RELIEFS, CLOUDED WITH MANGANESE-PURPLE UNDER THE
GLAZE. H. 8½ in. ABOUT 1750. *Victoria and Albert Museum*
See page 29

66. FIGURE OF A LADY DRINKING TEA. 'ASTBURY' TYPE. ABOUT 1745. H. 5¼ in. *Bedford, Cecil Higgins Museum*
See page 30

67. GROUP, A MAN AND WOMAN WITH A DOG. CREAM-COLOURED
WARE, TOUCHED WITH COLOURS UNDER THE GLAZE. H. $8\frac{1}{4}$ in.
ABOUT 1755. *Victoria and Albert Museum*
See page 31

68. MILKING GROUP. EARTHENWARE, MOTTLED WITH MAN-
GANESE-PURPLE, GREEN AND BLUE UNDER A DEEP STRAW-
COLOURED GLAZE. H. 8½ in. ABOUT 1755.
Cambridge, Fitzwilliam Museum
See page 31

69. EQUESTRIAN GROUP. CREAM-COLOURED WARE, MOTTLED
WITH BROWN, GREEN AND GREY UNDER THE GLAZE. H. $7\frac{1}{2}$ in.
ABOUT 1740. *Brighton Museum*
See page 30

70. FIGURE OF A CHINAMAN ON A BUFFALO. 'TORTOISESHELL
WARE', CLOUDED WITH MANGANESE-PURPLE UNDER THE GLAZE.
H. 6¾ in. ABOUT 1750. *Victoria and Albert Museum*
See page 31

71. FIGURE OF AN ELEPHANT. CREAM-COLOURED WARE, SPLASHED WITH BLACK AND MANGANESE-PURPLE UNDER THE GLAZE. H. $3\frac{7}{8}$ in. ABOUT 1750. *British Museum*
See page 31

72A. TEAPOT. WHITE SALTGLAZE WARE, PAINTED IN ENAMEL
COLOURS IN IMITATION OF JAPANESE KAKIEMON PORCELAIN.
ABOUT 1750. H. 5¾ in. *British Museum*
See page 32

72B. MILK-JUG. WHITE SALTGLAZE WARE, CAST WITH RELIEF
ORNAMENT AND PAINTED IN ENAMEL COLOURS WITH CHINESE
FLOWERS AND A BUST OF PRINCE CHARLES EDWARD, THE
YOUNG PRETENDER. ABOUT 1745. H. 5½ in.
Bedford, Cecil Higgins Museum
See page 32

73. MUG. WHITE SALTGLAZE WARE, PAINTED IN ENAMEL
COLOURS WITH CHINESE FIGURES. H. $6\frac{1}{8}$ in.
Cambridge, Fitzwilliam Museum
See page 32

74. JUG. WHITE SALTGLAZE WARE, PAINTED IN ENAMEL
COLOURS WITH FLOWERS AND THE INITIALS T B AND DATE 1762.
H. 6¾ in. *Victoria and Albert Museum*
See page 32

75. JUG. WHITE SALTGLAZE WARE, PAINTED IN ENAMEL COLOURS
WITH A PORTRAIT OF JOHN WALTER, OF CHECKLEY, STAFFS.; IN
HIS HAND A BOOK ENTITLED 'ART OF FARRIERY'. UNDER THE
BASE A DEDICATION FROM THE REV. J. MIDDLETON, CURATE
OF HANLEY. DATED 1768. H. $6\frac{7}{8}$ in.
Stoke-on-Trent, Hanley Museum and Art Gallery

See page 33

76. COFFEE-POT. WHITE SALTGLAZE WARE, COATED WITH BLUE
SLIP AND PAINTED OVER IT IN OPAQUE WHITE AND BLACK
ENAMELS. H. 8 in. ABOUT 1755. *Victoria and Albert Museum*
See page 34

77. JUG. WHITE SALTGLAZE WARE, PAINTED IN ENAMEL
COLOURS. INSCRIBED: *Thoˢ Allsop.* H. 8¾ in. ABOUT 1765.
Victoria and Albert Museum
See page 32

78. TEAPOT. WHITE SALTGLAZE WARE, PAINTED IN ENAMEL
COLOURS. ON ONE SIDE A LADY DANCING, ON THE OTHER A MAN
SMOKING. H. 3¾ in. ABOUT 1765.
Stoke-on-Trent, Hanley Museum and Art Gallery
See page 33

79. TEAPOT. WHITE SALTGLAZE WARE. PAINTED IN PURPLE
ENAMEL TO IMITATE ENCRINILE LIMESTONE. H. 4⅛ in. ABOUT
1760. *Stoke-on-Trent, Hanley Museum and Art Gallery*
See page 33

80. PLATE. WHITE SALTGLAZE WARE. MOULDED IN RELIEF
AND PAINTED IN ENAMEL COLOURS. DIAM. $9\frac{1}{2}$ in. ABOUT 1760.

Mr and Mrs J. E. Lowy

See page 33

81. TEAPOT. WHITE SALTGLAZE WARE, WITH APPLIED RELIEF
DECORATION PAINTED IN ENAMEL COLOURS. H. $4\frac{1}{2}$ in. ABOUT
1755. *Cambridge, Fitzwilliam Museum*
See page 33

82. TEAPOT. WHITE SALTGLAZE WARE, PAINTED IN ENAMEL
COLOURS ON ONE SIDE WITH A FORTUNE-TELLER, ON THE
OTHER WITH A MAN CARRYING A BASKET. H. $4\frac{7}{8}$ in. ABOUT 1760.
British Museum
See page 33

83. TEAPOT. WHITE SALTGLAZE WARE, WITH APPLIED RELIEFS
TOUCHED WITH ENAMEL COLOURS. ON EACH SIDE A FIGURE OF
BACCHUS. H. $4\frac{1}{8}$ in. ABOUT 1750. *British Museum*
See page 33

84. PUNCH-BOWL. EARTHENWARE, PAINTED IN SLATE-BLUE,
INSIDE WITH THE FALL AND OTHER BIBLICAL SUBJECTS AND A
HORSEMAN, OUTSIDE WITH CHINESE LANDSCAPES, IN PANELS
RESERVED ON A GROUND SPRAYED WITH MANGANESE-PURPLE,
UNDER A DEEP STRAW-YELLOW GLAZE. INSCRIBED UNDER THE
BASE WITH INITIALS AND DATE: *E. B.* 1743. DIAM. 10 in.
British Museum
See page 34

85. Jug. EARTHENWARE, PAINTED IN UNDERGLAZE BLUE. IN-
SCRIBED: *Thoṣ Latham Chebsey* 1790. H. 10 in.
Stoke-on-Trent, Hanley Museum and Art Gallery
See page 35

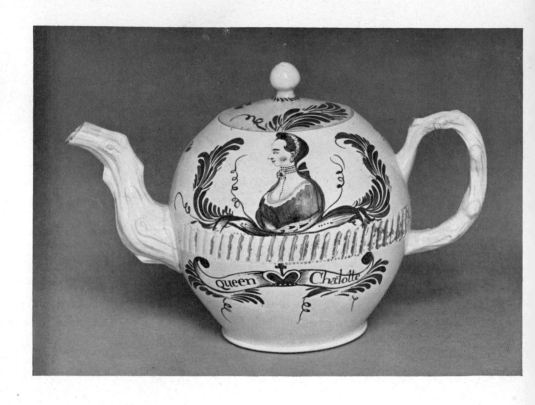

·86. TEAPOT. CREAM WARE. PAINTED IN ENAMEL COLOURS; ON
ONE SIDE A BUST OF QUEEN CHARLOTTE, ON THE OTHER A VIEW
OF A CHURCH. H. 5½ in. ABOUT 1761.
Cambridge, Fitzwilliam Museum
See page 35

87. TEAPOT. CREAM WARE, PAINTED IN RED AND BLACK ENAMEL
COLOURS. ON ONE SIDE A BIRD, ON THE OTHER FLOWERS.
H. 5¾ in. ABOUT 1765-1770. *Mr and Mrs J. E. Lowy*
See page 35

88. LOVING-CUP. CREAM WARE, PAINTED IN BRIGHT GREEN
AND RED. ON ONE SIDE A VIEW OF A HOUSE, ON THE OTHER THE
INITIALS AND DATE: *A. H.* 1772. H. $5\frac{1}{8}$ in.
Stoke-on-Trent, Hanley Museum and Art Gallery
See page 35

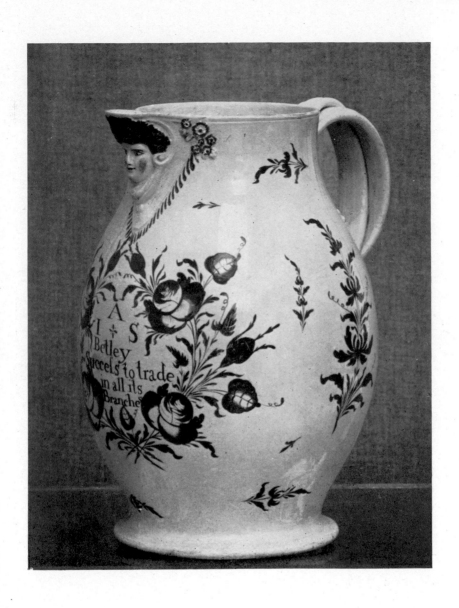

89. JUG. CREAM WARE, PAINTED IN RED, BLACK AND GREEN;
ON THE FRONT THE INSCRIPTION: *I^AS Betley Success to trade in all
its branches.* H. 9 in. ABOUT 1770. *Mr J. L. Dixon*
See page 36

90. FIGURE OF A SHEPHERD. EARTHENWARE PAINTED IN COLOURED GLAZES. MADE BY RALPH WOOD THE ELDER FROM A MODEL BY JOHN VOYEZ. H. 8$\frac{7}{8}$ in. ABOUT 1770.
Victoria and Albert Museum

See page 37

91. FIGURE, 'THE LOST PIECE OF SILVER'. EARTHENWARE
PAINTED IN COLOURED GLAZES. MADE BY RALPH WOOD THE
ELDER FROM A MODEL BY JOHN VOYEZ. H. 8 in. ABOUT 1770.
Cambridge, Fitzwilliam Museum
See pages 37, 38

92. FIGURE OF A DEER. EARTHENWARE PAINTED IN COLOURED
GLAZES. MADE BY RALPH WOOD THE ELDER FROM A MODEL
BY JOHN VOYEZ. H. $4\frac{1}{2}$ in. ABOUT 1770. *Victoria and Albert Museum*
See page 38

93. FIGURE OF A FOX WITH A CHICKEN. EARTHENWARE PAINTED
IN COLOURED GLAZES. MADE BY RALPH WOOD THE ELDER
FROM A MODEL BY JOHN VOYEZ. H. $4\frac{7}{8}$ in. ABOUT 1770.
Victoria and Albert Museum
See page 38

94. FIGURE OF A GIRL DANCING. EARTHENWARE PAINTED IN
ENAMEL COLOURS. MADE BY RALPH WOOD THE YOUNGER. H.
10⅜ in. ABOUT 1780. *Victoria and Albert Museum*
See page 38

95. FIGURES. EARTHENWARE PAINTED IN ENAMEL COLOURS. A, B
APOLLO AND CERES. MARK ON BOTH: C UNDER A CROWN, IM-
PRESSED. H. $6\frac{1}{4}$ in., $6\frac{1}{8}$ in. MADE AT HANLEY BY DAVID WILSON
FROM MODELS BY HENRY NEALE. ABOUT 1790.
Cambridge, Fitzwilliam Museum.
C, D WINTER AND SPRING, FROM A SET OF THE SEASONS. MARK
(ON SPRING): NEALE & CO. IMPRESSED. H. (BOTH) $5\frac{1}{2}$ in. MADE AT
HANLEY BY HENRY NEALE. ABOUT 1780.
Victoria and Albert Museum

See page 38

96. DISH. EARTHENWARE WITH APPLIED RELIEFS PAINTED IN
COLOURS. L. 14½ in. ABOUT 1790. *Victoria and Albert Museum*
See page 38